D0172404

Organ Donation

Margaret Haerens, Book Editor

GREENHAVEN PRESS
A part of Gale, Cengage Learning

GALE
CENGAGE Learning·

Detroit • New York • San Francisco • New Haven, Conn • Waterville, Maine • London

Elizabeth Des Chenes, *Director, Publishing Solutions*

© 2013 Greenhaven Press, a part of Gale, Cengage Learning

Gale and Greenhaven Press are registered trademarks used herein under license.

For more information, contact:
Greenhaven Press
27500 Drake Rd.
Farmington Hills, MI 48331-3535
Or you can visit our Internet site at gale.cengage.com

ALL RIGHTS RESERVED.
No part of this work covered by the copyright herein may be reproduced, transmitted, stored, or used in any form or by any means graphic, electronic, or mechanical, including but not limited to photocopying, recording, scanning, digitizing, taping, Web distribution, information networks, or information storage and retrieval systems, except as permitted under Section 107 or 108 of the 1976 United States Copyright Act, without the prior written permission of the publisher.

For product information and technology assistance, contact us at

Gale Customer Support, 1-800-877-4253
For permission to use material from this text or product, submit all requests online at
www.cengage.com/permissions

Further permissions questions can be emailed to permissionrequest@cengage.com

Articles in Greenhaven Press anthologies are often edited for length to meet page require-ments. In addition, original titles of these works are changed to clearly present the main thesis and to explicitly indicate the author's opinion. Every effort is made to ensure that Greenhaven Press accurately reflects the original intent of the authors. Every effort has been made to trace the owners of copyrighted material.

Cover image © Andia/Alamy.

LIBRARY OF CONGRESS CATALOGING-IN-PUBLICATION DATA

Organ donation / Margaret Haerens, book editor.
    p. cm. -- (Global viewpoints)
    Includes bibliographical references and index.
    ISBN 978-0-7377-6269-3 (hardcover) -- ISBN 978-0-7377-6445-1 (pbk.)
    1. Donation of organs, tissues, etc. 2. Donation of organs, tissues, etc.--Moral and ethical aspects. I. Haerens, Margaret.
    RD129.5O7382 2012
    362.17'83--dc23

                                       2012015585

Printed in the United States of America
2 3 4 5 6   18 17 16 15 14

Contents

Chapter 1: Organ Donation Worldwide

   A vigorous organ donation trade has sprouted up in
   many parts of the world in places where organs are
   scarce. In such situations, patients in more developed
   countries are exploiting men and women in lesser developed countries by paying for organs. Other countries
   have fostered a booming organ tourism trade, in which
   rich patients can visit and have organ transplants.

   Statistics show that Spain leads the world in organ donations. Experts attribute the country's success to its adoption of a presumed consent law and a nationwide coordination network that identifies potential donors. Other
   countries look to emulate Spain's accomplishments.

   Australia has a low rate of organ donation despite government efforts to raise awareness of the problem. The
   situation is so dire in the case of heart transplants that
   doctors are relying more and more on artificial hearts.

   Kuwait has a high rate of organ donations in relation to
   other Middle Eastern countries but still trails the United
   States and Europe. Officials contend that there is still a
   way to go to educate and raise awareness about the need
   for organ donation and to counter religious and cultural
   myths that hinder people's willingness to donate.

Chapter 2: Barriers to Organ Donation

Many Americans express reluctance to register as organ donors because of misconceptions about religious teachings about death. In some communities, there are cultural myths that persist about organ and tissue donation. It is important to be sensitive to these issues in any attempt to raise awareness about the practice of organ donation.

Religious and cultural myths against the practice of organ donations persist in Saudi Arabia. As a result, there is a dire shortage of organs for transplant, and the patients who can afford it go overseas where there are available organs. There is a renewed effort to address these issues.

Chapter 3: Strategies to Improve Organ Donations

Chapter 4: The Problem of Organ Trafficking

Foreword

*"The problems of all of humanity can
only be solved by all of humanity."*
—Swiss author Friedrich Dürrenmatt

Global interdependence has become an undeniable reality.
Mass media and technology have increased worldwide
access to information and created a society of global citizens.
Understanding and navigating this global community is a
challenge, requiring a high degree of information literacy and
a new level of learning sophistication.

Building on the success of its flagship series, Opposing
Viewpoints, Greenhaven Press has created the Global Viewpoints series to examine a broad range of current, often controversial topics of worldwide importance from a variety of
international perspectives. Providing students and other readers with the information they need to explore global connec-
tions and think critically about worldwide implications, each
Global Viewpoints volume offers a panoramic view of a topic
of widespread significance.

Drugs, famine, immigration—a broad, international treatment is essential to do justice to social, environmental, health,
and political issues such as these. Junior high, high school,
and early college students, as well as general readers, can all
use Global Viewpoints anthologies to discern the complexities
relating to each issue. Readers will be able to examine unique
national perspectives while, at the same time, appreciating the
interconnectedness that global priorities bring to all nations
and cultures.

Material in each volume is selected from a diverse range of
sources, including journals, magazines, newspapers, nonfiction
books, speeches, government documents, pamphlets, organiza-

tion newsletters, and position papers. Global Viewpoints is truly global, with material drawn primarily from international sources available in English and secondarily from US sources with extensive international coverage.

Features of each volume in the Global Viewpoints series include:

- An **annotated table of contents** that provides a brief summary of each essay in the volume, including the name of the country or area covered in the essay.

- An **introduction** specific to the volume topic.

- A **world map** to help readers locate the countries or areas covered in the essays.

- For each viewpoint, an **introduction** that contains notes about the author and source of the viewpoint explains why material from the specific country is being presented, summarizes the main points of the viewpoint, and offers three **guided reading questions** to aid in understanding and comprehension.

- **For further discussion** questions that promote critical thinking by asking the reader to compare and contrast aspects of the viewpoints or draw conclusions about perspectives and arguments.

- A worldwide list of **organizations to contact** for readers seeking additional information.

- A **periodical bibliography** for each chapter and a **bibliography of books** on the volume topic to aid in further research.

- A comprehensive **subject index** to offer access to people, places, events, and subjects cited in the text, with the countries covered in the viewpoints highlighted.

Global Viewpoints is designed for a broad spectrum of readers who want to learn more about current events, history, political science, government, international relations, economics, environmental science, world cultures, and sociology—students doing research for class assignments or debates, teachers and faculty seeking to supplement course materials, and others wanting to understand current issues better. By presenting how people in various countries perceive the root causes, current consequences, and proposed solutions to worldwide challenges, Global Viewpoints volumes offer readers opportunities to enhance their global awareness and their knowledge of cultures worldwide.

Introduction

"Every day, about 18 people in the United States die while waiting for an organ transplant. For people whose organs are failing because of disease or injury, donated organs and tissue may offer the gift of sight, freedom from machines, or even life itself."

—*University of Pittsburgh Medical Center (UPMC)*

The first known instance of human organ donation and transplantation was performed by Eduard Zirm, an Austrian ophthalmologist who successfully conducted a corneal tissue transplant on December 7, 1905. The donor was an eleven-year-old boy named Karl Brauer, whose eyes had been severely damaged in an accident. The recipient was a Czech farm laborer, Alois Glogar, who had been blinded in a fire. When Dr. Zirm realized that he would not be able to save Brauer's eyesight, he removed the boy's undamaged corneas and transplanted them onto Glogar's damaged ones. After only a few hours, Glogar regained vision in one of his eyes.

Zirm's achievement was an exciting step forward for transplantation science and inspired a number of other physicians to experiment with tissue, corneal, and organ transplantation. However, it became clear that corneal transplants were unique in that corneal procedures didn't encounter the problem that stumped scientists for years—tissue and organ rejection. As surgeons experimented with transplanting tissue and organs from donors, patients often died from the procedure because their bodies rejected the transplanted items. This was a difficult problem that took much scientific effort to solve.

Alexis Carrel, a French biologist and surgeon, did ground-breaking research into transplantation techniques, proving that blood vessels could be kept in cold storage for long periods of time before being used in transplant surgery. He also worked on transplanting whole organs and, in collaboration with legendary airman Charles Lindbergh, created a machine that provided a sterile respiratory system to organs removed from the body. These were important steps in developing the knowledge and techniques to preserving organ donations outside of the body and ultimately conducting successful transplant procedures.

More groundbreaking work in the transplantation field was done during World War I, when a pioneering surgeon named Harold Gillies made major steps in skin transplantation.

Yet, the obstacle of skin, tissue, and organ rejection remained a formidable one throughout the early twentieth century, as scientists experimented with various techniques to address the life-threatening problem. In 1936 a Russian surgeon, Yu Yu Voronoy, attempted the first human-to-human kidney transplant. After two days, the patient died because the body rejected the transplanted organ.

Progress in tackling the complicated problem was made by the Brazilian British surgeon Peter Medawar and Australian virologist Frank Burnet in the mid–twentieth century. They investigated the immunological processes underlying tissue rejection; in 1951 Medawar suggested that immunosuppressant drugs be used to counteract the body's immune system, which was responsible for rejecting donor tissue and organs. This discovery paved the way for organ transplantation to succeed and established the field of transplantation biology. Medawar and Burnet received Nobel Prizes for their work in 1960.

The first successful human-to-human kidney transplant occurred in 1954. Joseph E. Murray and a team of top surgeons in Boston transplanted a kidney between twenty-three-year-old identical twins, who went on to live long, healthy lives. This milestone proved to be an inspiration for transplant surgeons, some of whom began to develop the potential of using tissue and organs from the deceased in transplant procedures. In 1962 surgeons implanted the kidney from a dead donor into a live patient, using immunosuppressive drugs to treat organ rejection initiated by the patient's immune system. It worked, and the patient survived for twenty-one months. A year later, Dr. James Hardy implanted a lung from a deceased donor into a patient suffering from lung cancer in Jackson, Mississippi. The patient survived for eighteen days, eventually dying from kidney failure. In 1966 surgeons at the University of Minnesota performed the first successful pancreas transplant using the organ of a deceased donor. A year later, Dr. Thomas Starzl at the University of Colorado coordinated a successful liver transplant, allowing the patient to live another thirteen months.

Also in 1967, the world was captivated by another landmark transplantation surgery. At a hospital in Cape Town, South Africa, Dr. Christiaan Barnard and his transplant team were the first to conduct a successful human heart transplant. The donor was Denise Darvall, a twenty-three-year-old woman who died in a car accident; the recipient was fifty-four-year-old Louis Washkansky, a man dying from congestive heart failure. Although the surgery itself was a success, Washkansky died eighteen days later from pneumonia because of his weakened immune system.

The amount of publicity generated by the first heart transplant was extensive. Critics viewed it as a spectacle, an unfortunate and embarrassing circus that violated the privacy of both Darvall and Washkansky and made Barnard into a worldwide celebrity. Others regarded the publicity as a tool to raise awareness of the emerging field of transplantation biology and the promise that was being fulfilled by the talented doctors and surgical teams that were working to save lives. Supporters hoped that the publicity would inspire more young men and women to enter the field and lead to organ transplantation becoming more commonplace and effective in the years to come.

Today, organ transplantation has become a widely performed surgery. One necessary factor in facilitating its growth and success has been the establishment of organ procurement organizations (OPOs), which are nonprofit organizations that help to coordinate the process of organ donations. OPOs identify, procure, and allocate organs to patients who need them the most within their designated areas.

Another factor has been the introduction of donor cards, which indicate that an individual consents to donate his or her organs in case of death. In 1971 Great Britain introduced the first donor cards—a development that soon spread to other countries.

In the decades since the first successful heart transplant, medical science has made great leaps in developing new transplant surgeries. The first hand transplant occurred in France in 1998. The first successful partial face transplant took place in 2005; five years later, the first full face transplant was performed by a surgical team in Spain. In 2011 the first double-leg transplant took place in Spain.

Yet as tissue and organ transplantation becomes a viable option for more and more people around the world, the supply of organs has not kept up with the demand. In most countries, there are more people in need of organs than there are those donating organs. A robust black market has emerged, and organ trafficking has become a serious problem in many parts of the world.

The authors of the viewpoints in *Global Viewpoints: Organ Donation* explore key issues associated with the state of organ donation around the world today, including the pressing demand for donated organs; various organ donation policies and systems in different countries; and the pernicious and enduring crime of organ trafficking, a practice that preys on the poor and vulnerable in many countries. The viewpoints provide insight into strategies and policies that are being utilized to raise awareness and improve rates of organ donation, as well as address organ trafficking in nations and communities around the globe.

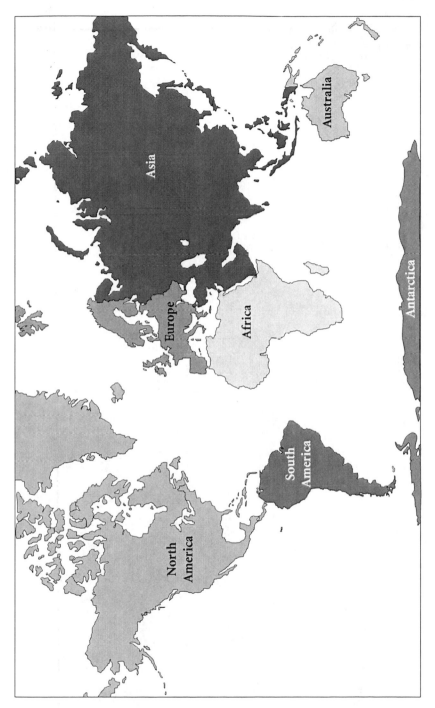

GLOBALVIEWPOINTS

Organ Donation Worldwide

The State of the International Organ Trade: A Provisional Picture Based on Integration of Available Information

Yosuke Shimazono

Yosuke Shimazono was a researcher and student at the Institute of Social and Cultural Anthropology at the University of Oxford. In the following viewpoint, he surveys the state of organ transplantation around the world, finding that it varies according to factors such as the level of health care, technological ability, and the availability of organs. Shimazono notes that an international organ trade has emerged, one that preys on the poor and vulnerable and supplies organs to the wealthy in developed countries. He argues that these global inequities should be considered a global public health issue and should be addressed by international, national, and regional authorities. Shimazono maintains that there is also an urgent need for more research on the problem.

As you read, consider the following questions:

1. According to the World Health Organization (WHO), how many countries perform kidney transplants?

Yosuke Shimazono, "The State of the International Organ Trade: A Provisional Picture Based on Integration of Available Information," *Bulletin of the World Health Organization*, vol. 85, no. 12, December 2007, pp. 901–980. Copyright © 2007 by the World Health Organization. All rights reserved. Reproduced by permission.

2. According to the Voluntary Health Association of India, how many Indians sell a kidney every year?

3. According to a report by Organs Watch, what countries are identified as organ-importing countries?

Introduction

Organ transplantation is an effective therapy for end-stage organ failure and is widely practised around the world. According to WHO, kidney transplants are carried out in 91 countries. Around 66,000 kidney transplants, 21,000 liver transplants and 6,000 heart transplants were performed globally in 2005. The access of patients to organ transplantation, however, varies according to their national situations, and is partly determined by the cost of health care, the level of technical capacity and, most importantly, the availability of organs.

The shortage of organs is virtually a universal problem. In some countries, the development of a deceased organ donation programme is hampered by sociocultural, legal and other factors. Even in developed countries, where rates of deceased organ donation tend to be higher than in other countries, organs from this source fail to meet the increasing demand. The use of live donors for kidney and liver transplantation is also practised, but the purchase and sale of transplant organs from live donors are prohibited in many countries.[1]

The shortage of an indigenous "supply" of organs has led to the development of the international organ trade, where potential recipients travel abroad to obtain organs through commercial transactions. The international organ trade has been recognized as a significant health policy issue in the international community. A World Health Assembly resolution adopted in 2004 (WHA 57.18) urges member states to "take measures to protect the poorest and vulnerable groups from 'transplant tourism' and the sale of tissues and organs".[2] Despite growing awareness of the issue, the reality of the international organ trade is not well understood due to a paucity of data and also a lack of effort to integrate the available information.

This paper is a preliminary attempt to bring together the available information on the international organ trade. It aims to present a tentative global picture of the context and forms of the organ trade; the major organ-exporting and -importing countries; and the outcomes and consequences of commercial organ transplants.

The international organ trade has been recognized as a significant health policy issue in the international community.

Methods

This paper originated from a literature review commissioned by the Clinical Procedures Unit of WHO's Department of Essential Health Technologies and was undertaken during July and August 2006. Its purpose was to gather information on the international organ trade and transplant tourism, and to synthesize this into a tentative global picture using multiple research strategies.

Medical articles on the outcome of commercially arranged overseas transplants were collected through Medline/PubMed. Using Reference Manager, the first search was conducted using two parameters: "kidney transplantation" AND "nonrelated" OR "unrelated"; the second search was made with "kidney transplantation" AND "commerce" OR "commercial". The abstracts were checked and, if judged relevant, the entire items were retrieved; their references were also consulted. Academic articles containing information on the scope and trends of the international organ trade were obtained using the same search procedure.

Because the paucity of scientific research was anticipated, media reports were identified as significant complementary resources. Articles published in the past five years that were accessible in both English and Japanese were examined. The initial search was made using online database services [Lexis-Nexis Global Business and News Service, accessed through Oxford University Library Services (OXLIP; availabale at: http://www.bodley.ox.ac.uk/oxlip/index.html)]. Articles indexed as "organ trafficking" were examined and items containing factual information on the organ trade were retrieved. After the identification of the major "organ importing and exporting" countries, reiterative searches were made to gather further information from the aforementioned database and Google searches. Relevant items in the author's personal library were also included. For the purpose of this paper, an additional survey of media reports published up to 10 May 2007 was carried out. A summary of the survey was presented at the second global consultation on human transplantation at WHO's Geneva headquarters (28–30 May 2007), and benefited from the participants' comments and information.

The material obtained using these methods was organized into a searchable database and systematically reviewed.

Results

In total, 309 documents—243 media materials, 51 journal articles and 15 other documents—were judged to be the most relevant. As anticipated, quantitative data was scarce. However, several documents, including academic articles, conference papers and reports by health ministries and national transplant registries, were obtained for several countries. Media reports were found to be useful in gaining information on the prevalence and forms of the international organ trade and as a source of data not accessible in academic journals. The major findings from these will be summarized below.

Forms of the International Organ Trade

Transplant Tourism The most common way to trade organs across national borders is via potential recipients who travel abroad to undergo organ transplantation, commonly referred to as "transplant tourism", although this term may be contentious as it disregards the patients' desperate motives and fails to reflect ethical issues. However, it is used in resolution WHA 57.18 and in international health policy discussion to refer to overseas transplantation when a patient obtains an organ through the organ trade or other means that contravene the regulatory frameworks of their countries of origin.

"Transplant tourism" involves not only the purchase and sale of organs, but also other elements relating to the commercialization of organ transplantation. The international movement of potential recipients is often arranged or facilitated by intermediaries and health-care providers who arrange the travel and recruit donors. The Internet has often been used to attract foreign patients. Several web sites offer all-inclusive "transplant packages"—the price of a renal transplant package ranges from US$70,000 to 160,000 (Table 1 [not shown]).

There are also facilitators in the recipients' countries of origin. In Taiwan, China, 118 patients who underwent organ transplants in China were questioned by their department of health, and 69 reported that their transplants were facilitated by doctors. Subsequently, the local authorities in Taiwan, China, have prohibited such activities.[3] There have also been allegations that embassy officials of certain Middle Eastern countries have facilitated overseas commercial kidney transplants in Pakistan and the Philippines.[4, 5]

Under the General Agreement on Trade in Services (GATS), governments may choose to trade health services to achieve their national health objectives. Health service exports, through the treatment of foreign patients entering their territory (classified as "mode 2" or "consumption abroad"), are used by some countries as an instrument of economic development.[6] The trade in transplant-related health services across borders, however, may result in the inequitable allocation of deceased donor organs and has also raised ethical concerns, especially when this occurs in a country where the regulatory frameworks to protect live organ donors from coercion, exploitation and physical harm are not well developed or implemented.

"Transplant tourism" involves not only the purchase and sale of organs, but also other elements relating to the commercialization of organ transplantation.

Other Forms of International Organ Trade There are other forms of international organ trade that demand attention. In some cases, live donors have reportedly been brought from the Republic of Moldova to the United States of America, or from Nepal to India.[7, 8] In other cases, both recipients and donors from different countries move to a third country. More than 100 illegal kidney transplants were performed at St. Augustine's Hospital in South Africa in 2001 and 2002; most of the recipients came from Israel, while the donors were from eastern Europe and Brazil. The police investigation in Brazil and South Africa revealed the existence of an international organ trafficking syndicate.[9] These cases may involve human trafficking for the purpose of organ transplantation. Unlike cell tissues, no confirmed report on transplant organs being trafficked after their removal was found in this survey.

The Organ-Exporting Countries

India was a commonly known organ-exporting country, where organs from local donors are regularly transplanted to foreigners through sale and purchase. Although the number of foreign recipients seems to have decreased after the enactment of a law banning the organ trade (the Transplantation of Human Organs Act of 1994),[10] the underground organ market is still existent and resurging in India. The Voluntary Health Association of India estimates that about 2,000 Indians sell a

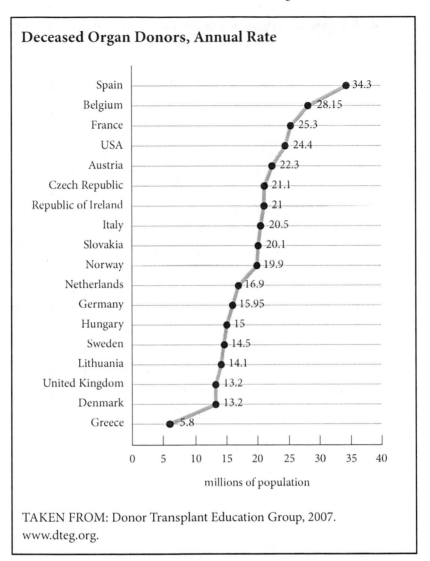

Deceased Organ Donors, Annual Rate

Country	Rate
Spain	34.3
Belgium	28.15
France	25.3
USA	24.4
Austria	22.3
Czech Republic	21.1
Republic of Ireland	21
Italy	20.5
Slovakia	20.1
Norway	19.9
Netherlands	16.9
Germany	15.95
Hungary	15
Sweden	14.5
Lithuania	14.1
United Kingdom	13.2
Denmark	13.2
Greece	5.8

millions of population

TAKEN FROM: Donor Transplant Education Group, 2007. www.dteg.org.

kidney every year.[11] The drop in foreign recipients in India was accompanied by an increase in the number of foreign recipients in other countries, such as Pakistan and the Philippines.

In Pakistan, according to the Sindh Institute of Urology, approximately 2,000 renal transplants were performed in 2005, of which up to two-thirds were estimated to have been performed on foreigners.[12] In the Philippines, data obtained from the Renal Disease Control Program of the National Kidney Transplant Institute, show that of the 468 kidney transplants in 2003, 110 were for patients from abroad. There is no comparable data for Egypt but a considerable number of patients from neighbouring countries are believed to undergo organ transplantation there.[13]

In China, around 12,000 kidney and liver transplants were performed in 2005. Most of the transplant organs were alleged to have been procured from executed prisoners, a practice which itself is criticized by the international community.[14, 15] In the absence of paid organ donors, a question may be raised regarding whether the deceased organ transplants in China constitute an organ trade. Yet the lack of established rules about the allocation of organs, coupled with the prioritizing of foreigners due to their ability to pay and the existence of brokers, have been widely reported. These factors have led to the view that deceased organ transplants for foreigners in China do constitute part of the international organ trade. The number of foreign recipients in China is difficult to estimate, but a media report offers circumstantial evidence that over half of the 900 kidney and liver transplants performed in one major transplant centre in 2004 were for non-Chinese citizens from 19 countries.[16]

The lack or insufficiency of a legal framework or enforcing mechanism in these countries has been highlighted by the public media and local experts. However, the Chinese and Pakistani governments recently have been taking steps to curtail the international organ trade (as of May 2007), which may change their respective situations.[17, 18]

Other countries where kidneys are reportedly sold include Bolivia, Brazil, Iraq, Israel, the Republic of Moldova, Peru and Turkey.[19] In Colombia, where 69 of 873 organ transplants were performed on foreigners, there is an allegation that organs of deceased donors were used in the organ transplants that were commercially arranged for foreigners.[20] The case of the Islamic Republic of Iran merits a special mention: Paid kidney donation is practised legally but there is a strict regulation of the allocation of organs to non-local citizens, thereby restricting the international organ trade.[21] In contrast, the Philippine government is moving towards institutionalization of paid kidney donation and acceptance of foreign patients.[4]

The Organ-Importing Countries

The term "organ-importing countries" is used here to refer to the countries of origin of the patients going overseas to purchase organs for transplantation. A report by Organs Watch, an organization based at the University of California, USA, identified Australia, Canada, Israel, Japan, Oman, Saudi Arabia and the USA as major organ-importing countries.[19]

Yet transplant tourism has become prevalent in many other countries of all continents and regions. Data are available through surveys conducted by health authorities and professional societies in these regions (Table 2 [not shown]). It should be noted that in some countries the number of patients going overseas for kidney transplantation outweighs the number of patients undergoing kidney transplantation locally. More detailed data available from Malaysia and Oman show the shifting destinations of overseas organ transplantation (Fig. 1, Fig. 2 and Table 3 [not shown]).

Although it is premature to undertake a substantial analysis of this issue because comparable data from other regions are not available, these data suggest a heavier reliance on overseas transplantation and transplant tourism in Asia and the Middle East than in other regions. For example, in Canada and the United Kingdom (where, respectively, 1027 and 1914 domestic renal transplants were performed in 2005)[26, 27] it is estimated by local experts that around 30 to 50 patients undergo overseas commercial kidney transplants.[28, 29]

Consequences and Effects

In several instances, newspaper articles have reported the deaths of patients who went abroad for overseas commercial transplants; the abuse, fraud and coercion of paid kidney donors are also frequently reported. These reports have raised serious concerns about the consequences of the international organ trade, both for recipients and donors.

The studies on the outcomes of kidney transplants performed for non-local residents in organ-importing countries are summarized in Table 3 [not shown].[30-42] In some studies, mostly those based on small data sets, patient survival and graft survival rates are considerably lower than the internationally accepted standard; in other studies, they are shown to be comparable with local results. Confounding factors—e.g., survivor biases, locations, periods and number of data sets— make generalizations difficult.

In several instances, newspaper articles have reported the deaths of patients who went abroad for overseas commercial transplants; the abuse, fraud and coercion of paid kidney donors are also frequently reported.

Many of these studies, nonetheless, report a heightened frequency of medical complications, including the transmission of HIV and the hepatitis B and C viruses.[30-41] Moreover, one study from the United Kingdom reports that patients who had been suspended from the local transplant list for medical reasons were operated on abroad.[33] These factors seem to indicate the existence of substandard medical practices. Given the desperate desire of the patients to undergo organ transplantation, their risk of being exploited should not be underestimated.

Even less empirical research has investigated the health and other impacts of paid organ donation on the donors. No medical data about the health status of paid kidney donors were found in this survey.

Several social scientific studies described the perceived health and economic status effects of kidney donation on paid donors in certain countries. Three quantitative data sets are summarized in Table 4 [not shown]. This research shows that the underlying motivation of most paid kidney donors is poverty, and that lasting economic benefit after donation is limited or even negative because of the limited employability of such patients and the perceived deterioration of their health. Results from other more qualitative research are consistent with these quantitative surveys in other countries. Paid kidney donation is also associated with depression, regret and discrimination. Paid kidney donors do not receive follow-up care, due to financial and other reasons.[43-48]

Discussion

The results of this survey suggest that the international organ trade no longer represents sporadic instances in transplant medicine. In view of the circumstantial evidence cited, the total number of recipients who underwent commercial organ transplants overseas may be conservatively estimated at around 5% of all recipients in 2005. Moreover, undergoing transplantation through the international organ trade has become the most common way of undergoing organ transplantation in certain countries.

The international organ trade links the incapacity of national health care systems to meet the needs of patients with the lack of appropriate regulatory frameworks or implementation elsewhere. It exploits these discrepancies and is based on global inequities. Accordingly, the growth and regularization of the international organ trade should be regarded as a global public health issue.

Health authorities have been urged to update their legal frameworks—in both organ-exporting and -importing countries. Yet they must also address the underlying problem of organ shortage by using organs from ethically acceptable sources. International cooperation may be considered to establish rules pertaining to overseas transplantation to curtail the international organ trade. While considerable disagreement exists over whether the legally regulated market and the use of financial rewards and incentives are ethically acceptable, the *international* organ trade could be an issue on which international consensus and policy harmonization could be effectively pursued.

This survey of the international organ trade is limited in several ways, reflecting the scarcity of previous efforts to gather and synthesize the relevant information. The picture of the international organ trade presented in this paper should be regarded as provisional and tentative. One conclusion is that there is an urgent need for further medical and social scientific research. The paucity of previous efforts to monitor the international organ trade arguably indicates an inadequate current mechanism to deal effectively with this global issue. Establishing a platform on which researchers, policy makers, professional societies and international governing bodies cooperate in gathering and sharing information may be considered an essential step towards a more substantial international health policy.

References

1. Cherry MJ. *Kidney for sale by owner: human organs, transplantation, and the market.* Washington: Georgetown University Press; 2005.

2. *Resolution on human organ and tissue transplantation.* Geneva: WHO; 2004 (WHA 57.18). Available at: http://www.who.int/transplantation/en/A57_R18-en.pdf

3. Doctors banned from brokering transplants. *China Post.* 2006 Aug 17.

4. Endo F. Organ plan poses ethical issues; new RP scheme to allow kidney trading aims to close back market. *Daily Yomiuri.* 2007 Feb 3.

5. Walsh D. Transplant tourists flock to Pakistan, where poverty and lack of regulation fuels trade in human organs. *The Guardian*. 2005 Feb 10.

6. *WTO agreements and public health: a joint study by the WHO and the WTO secretariat*. Geneva: WHO, World Trade Organization; 2002.

7. Haviland C. Nepal's trade of doom. *BBC News*. 2004 Sep 21. Available at: http://news.bbc.co.uk/1/hi/world/south _asia/3674328.stm

8. Kates B. Black market in transplant organs, donors smuggled into US to sell body parts. *Daily News*. 2005 Aug 25.

9. McLaughlin A, Prusher IR, Downie A. What is a kidney worth? *Christian Science Monitor*. 2004 Jun 9.

10. *Transplantation of Human Organs Act*, India; 1994, Act No. 42.

11. Hogg C. Why not allow organ trading? *BBC News*. 2002 Aug 30. Available at: http://news.bbc.co.uk/1/hi/health/ 2224554.stm

12. Rizvi, A. *Pakistan: Legislative framework on transplantation. Second global consultation in human transplantation*. Geneva: WHO; 28–30 Mar 2007.

13. Egypt: Poverty pushes poor Egyptians to sell their organs. *IRIN*. 2006 May 30.

14. Minhua J, Yingguang Z. Beijing mulls new law on transplants of deathrow inmates organs. *Caijing*. 2005 Nov 28.

15. China at world advanced level in organ transplant. *People's Daily Online*. 2006 Jun 12. Available at: http:// english.people.com.cn/200606/12/eng20060612_273290 .html

16. Kim C. Tianjin, a transplant "mecca" that attracts patients from 19 Asian countries [Japanese text]. Chusonilbo. 2005 Jan 30. Available at: http://www.chosunonline.com/ article/20050130000046

17. Government open to suggestions on human organs ordinance. *Associated Press of Pakistan.* 2007 Feb 24.

18. New regulations banning trade of human organs go into effect. *Xinhua General News Service.* 2007 May 1; Sect. Domestic News.

19. Scheper-Hughes N. Prime numbers: organs without borders. *Foreign Policy* 200529-31.

20. Fabregas L. Transplant 'tourism' questioned at medical centers in Colombia. *Pittsburgh Tribune Review.* 2007 Feb 18.

21. Ghods AJ, Nasrollahzadeh D. Transplant tourism and the Iranian model of renal transplantation program: ethical considerations. *Exp Clin Transplant* 2005; 3: 351-4.

22. Growing number of Koreans getting organ transplants in China. *Chusonilbo.* 2004 Oct 24. Available at: http://english.chosun.com/w21data/html/news/200410/200410 240016.html

23. National Transplant Registry M. *First Report of the National Transplant Registry Malaysia 2004.* Kuala Lumpur: National Transplant Registry; 2005. Available at: http:// www.mst.org.my/ntrSite/publications_1stReport2004.htm

24. Mohsin N. Transplantation in Saudi Arabia and Oman. Consultation on Cell, Tissue and Organ Transplantation; 2005 Nov 26-28; Karachi.

25. Annual Report. 2006. Saudi Center for Organ Transplantation: 2007. Available at: http://www.scot.org.sa/annual-report.html

26. *Transplant activity report 2005-2006.* Transplant UK: 2007. Available at: http://www.uktransplant.org.uk/ukt/statistics/transplant_activity_report/transplant_activity_report.jsp

27. *Preliminary statistics on organ donation, transplantation and waiting list: 2007.* Canadian Organ Replacement Register: 2007. Available at: http://secure.cihi.ca/cihiweb/dispPage.jsp?cw_page=services_corr_e#report

28. Jimenez M. B.C. Firm offers $75,000 kidneys in China: Critics outrage as clients pay to receive a transplant in just 15 days. *National Post.* 2003 Mar 18.

29. Dennis E. Dangers for travelling for transplants. *Press Association Newsfile.* 2006 Nov 27.

30. Akpolat T, Ozturk M. Commerce in renal transplantation. *Transplant Proc* 1998; 30: 710-1.

31. Al-Wakeel J, Mitwall AH, Tarif N, Malik GH, Al-Mohaya S, Alam A, et al. Living unrelated renal transplantation: outcome and issues. *Saudi Journal of Kidney Disease & Transplantation* 2000;11:553-8. Available at: http://www.sjkdt.org.sa/CMS400Min/uploadedFiles/Archive/Volume_11/Number_4_December_2005/Articles/05%20J.%20Wakeel.pdf

32. Frishberg Y, Feinstein S, Drukker A. Living unrelated (commercial) renal transplantation in children. *J Am Soc Nephrol* 1998; 9: 1100-3.

33. Inston NG, Gill D, Al-Hakim A, Ready AR. Living paid organ transplantation results in unacceptably high recipient morbidity and mortality. *Transplant Proc* 2005; 37: 560-2.

34. Ivanovski N, Popov Z, Cakalaroski K, Masin J, Spasovski G, Zafirovska K. Living-unrelated (paid) renal transplantation—ten years later. *Transplant Proc* 2005; 37: 563-4.

35. SE Kennedy, Y Shen, JA Charlesworth, Mackie JD, Mahony JD, Kelly JJ, et al., et al. Outcome of overseas commercial kidney transplantation: an Australian perspective. *Med J Aust* 2005; 182: 224-7.

36. The Living Non-related Renal Transplant Study Group. Commercially motivated renal transplantation: results in 540 patients transplanted in India. The Living Non-Related Renal Transplant Study Group. *Clin Transplant* 1997; 11: 536-44.

37. Morad Z, Lim TO. Outcome of overseas kidney transplantation in Malaysia. *Transplant Proc* 2000; 32: 1485-6.

38. Sever MS, Kazancioglu R, Yildiz A, Turkmen A, Ecder T, Kayacan SM, et al., et al. Outcome of living unrelated (commercial) renal transplantation. *Kidney Int* 2001; 60: 1477-83.

39. Ben Hamida F, Ben Abdallah T, Goucha R, Hedri H, Helal I, Karoui C, et al., et al. Outcome of living unrelated (commercial) renal transplantation: report of 20 cases. *Transplant Proc* 2001; 33: 2660-1.

40. Colakoglu M, Yenicesu M, Akpolat T, Vural A, Utas C, Arinsoy T, et al., et al. Nonrelated living-donor kidney transplantation: medical and ethical aspects. *Nephron* 1998; 79: 447-51.

41. Kucuk M, Sever MS, Turkmen A, Sahin S, Kazancioglu R, Ozturk S, et al., et al. Demographic analysis and outcome features in a transplant outpatient clinic. *Transplant Proc* 2005; 37: 743-6.

42. Sun CY, Lee CC, Chang CT, Hung CC, Wu MS. Commercial cadaveric renal transplant: an ethical rather than medical issue. *Clin Transplant* 2006; 20: 340-5.

43. Cohen L. Where it hurts: Indian material for an ethics of organ transplantation. *Daedalus* 1999; 128: 135-65.

44. Goyal M, Mehta RL, Schneiderman LJ, Sehgal AR. Economic and health consequences of selling a kidney in India. *JAMA* 2002; 288: 1589-93.

45. Scheper-Hughes N. Parts unknown: undercover ethnography of the organs-trafficking underworld. *Ethnography* 2004; 5: 29-73.

46. Zargooshi J. Iranian kidney donors: motivations and relations with recipients. *J Urol* 2001; 165: 386-92.

47. Zargooshi J. Quality of life of Iranian kidney "donors". *J Urol* 2001; 166: 1790-9.

48. Scheper-Hughes N. Keeping an eye on the global traffic in human organs. *Lancet* 2003; 361: 1645-8.

49. Budiani D. Consequences of living kidney donors in Egypt. *10th Congress of the Middle East Society for Organ Transplantation; 2006 Nov 26-29; Kuwait.*

Affiliations

a. Institute of Social and Cultural Anthropology, University of Oxford, Oxford, England.

Spain Leads the World in Organ Donations

Grace Wong

Grace Wong is a reporter for CNN. In the following viewpoint, she reports that the worldwide status of organ donations is largely determined by a country's policies on the issue. Spain, which implemented an implied consent system as well as a nationwide transplant coordination network, has been very effective in raising the rate of organ donations. Wong notes that a number of countries, including Britain, are looking to emulate Spain's success in this area.

As you read, consider the following questions:

1. According to Wong, how many deceased donors per million population does Spain have?
2. How many deceased donors per million population does Australia have?
3. What does Wong give as the Spanish conversion rate of donors?

Earlier this week [June 2009] the case of Hiroki Ando, the Japanese 11-year-old boy who was denied a heart transplant in Japan, highlighted the vast cultural divide in attitudes towards organ transplant and availability worldwide.

Grace Wong, "Spain Leads the Way in Organ Donations," CNN.com, June 17, 2009. Copyright © 2009 by CNN. All rights reserved. Reproduced by permission.

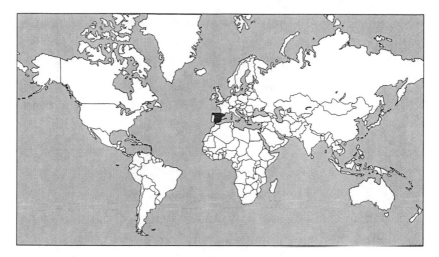

Hiroki had to travel to the U.S., where he is awaiting a heart, because Japan prohibits organ transplants involving children.

His story highlights the wide range of policies around the world regarding organ donation.

Organ donation has saved and improved countless lives. But medical advancements have led to a rise in demand for organs that is outpacing donation rates.

Some countries, particularly Spain, have succeeded in raising the number of organ donors, but there is still much room for improvement, according to Leo Roels, managing director of the Donor Action Foundation.

"What we see in our experience in so many countries is that there is still a lot of potential when it comes to identifying donors," he told CNN.

The Donor Action Foundation is a nonprofit group that helps hospitals implement programs designed to improve their donation rates. It's active in 17 countries worldwide.

Looking at deceased donors per million population—a commonly used benchmark—rates vary widely around the world.

Spain leads internationally with 34 deceased donors per million population, according to figures from the International Registry of Organ Donation and Transplantation.

Australia, on the other hand, noticeably lags countries with comparable health care systems with just 12 deceased donors per million population.

A variety of factors impact organ donation rates, from the legal environment to training to cultural obstacles, experts said.

In Japan, the law prevents children from donating organs, but there is also an overall reluctance to donate organs that is rooted in Shinto and Buddhist attitudes towards death.

Japan didn't legalize organ transplants from brain-dead donors until 1997, according to the Japan Organ Transplant Network, a nongovernmental group.

Organ donation has saved and improved countless lives. But medical advancements have led to a rise in demand for organs that is outpacing donation rates.

Although, the government is currently looking at changes to the law that could pave the way for more transplants.

"Even among medical professionals, the support for the concept of brain death in Japan is significantly lower than in European countries," Roels said.

Even in the U.S., which is one of the leading countries for organ donations, there are still some cultural obstacles and religious concerns about what constitutes death.

It's a mixed picture for donor rates in the U.S., according to Joel Newman of the United Network for Organ Sharing, which runs the country's only organ transplant network.

Deceased donor rates are well above levels from the late 1990s and early 2000s, but they have hit a plateau.

Spain's Success

Spain has about 5,500 people on the transplant waiting list, compared with about 8,000 in the UK [United Kingdom]. It has only two-thirds the UK population, but the impressive part is the proportion of families who say yes to organ donation at the moment of death. In the UK, it is 60%. In Spain, it is up to 85%. The organ donation rate in Spain is 34 per million. The latest figure for the UK is 15.5.

Sarah Boseley,
"Spain's Family Bonds Lie at the Heart and Soul
of Great Healthcare," Guardian, March 30, 2011.

"People in their own lifetime, even if they have positive feelings about organ donation, don't make a commitment," he said. "They don't fill out donor cards or have a conversation with their family."

Countries like Spain, Belgium and Norway have passed "presumed consent" laws where individuals are automatically considered an organ donor unless they opt out.

While these laws have helped improve rates of organ donation, success in countries like world leader Spain has largely been attributed to the organizational measures it has implemented.

Spain established a nationwide transplant coordination network in 1989 to help doctors and transplant coordinators to identify potential donors.

The so-called Spanish Model has achieved results such that its organizational measures have been recommended by the World Health Organization.

The UK [United Kingdom] is one country emulating aspects of the Spanish system. It's in the process of overhauling its transplant network in a bid to improve its effectiveness.

The percentage of potential donors who actually donate organs—a measure of the efficiency of a transplant network—is around 50 percent in the UK, according to Chris Rudge, the UK's national clinical director for transplantation.

By comparison, the Spanish system has a so-called conversion rate of 80 percent to 85 percent and the U.S. is targeting around 75 percent, he said.

"What we're trying to do in this country is change the attitude toward organ donation. At the moment it's unusual, and we want to make it usual," Rudge told CNN.

In the aims of getting more families to give consent, the UK is more than doubling the number of transplant coordinators in its hospitals to 250. Hospitals in the UK are required to obtain consent for organ donation from individuals or families.

These coordinators, who will receive specialized training to work with families and handle ethical issues, will team up with senior doctors in intensive care units of hospitals to identify potential donors. The framework for the collaborative program should be in place by April of next year [2010].

The presence of transplant coordinators is important, but it's just one of many measures that need to be taken in order to get a grip on the organ shortfall problem, Roels noted.

"There is a need to combine factors like training, education and better identification. It's a combination of these factors that will improve donor rates further," he said.

How to Mend a Broken Heart

Kate Benson

Kate Benson is a reporter for the Sydney Morning Herald. *In the following viewpoint, she reports that Australia's rate of organ donation is so low that many patients in need of heart transplants are turning to mechanical pumps and other technology to save their lives. Much of the money for such expensive devices is donated by benefactors, and many health officials in Australia are urging the government to provide more funding to help those who need artificial hearts. Although there are serious risks to using such devices, Benson continues, until Australia's heart donation rate improves it is the only viable solution some patients have.*

As you read, consider the following questions:

1. How many organ donors does Benson say that Australia has per every million people?
2. How many hearts were donated in Australia in 2009, according to the author?
3. According to Benson, how many Australians could receive an artificial heart if government funding was granted?

Kate Benson, "How to Mend a Broken Heart," *Sydney Morning Herald*, August 18, 2010. Copyright © 2010 Fairfax Media Syndication. All rights reserved. Reproduced by permission.

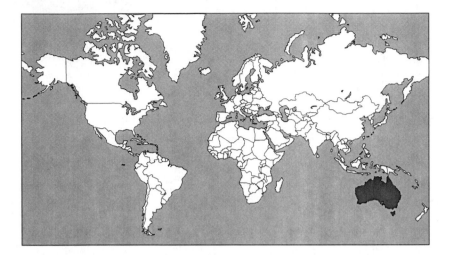

Being accused of having no ticker has always been a harsh insult. It paints a picture of someone quick to walk away from a challenge. But when Angelo Tigano was told he had two weeks to live, giving up was the last thing on his mind.

The 50-year-old from the Sydney suburb of Fairfield, who has idiopathic cardiomyopathy, found himself in the spotlight this week when he became the first person in the Southern Hemisphere to have surgery for a total, artificial heart—one that takes over the work of both his left and right ventricles.

The five-hour operation at St Vincent Hospital has also thrown new light on Australia's organ donation rate—still one of the lowest in the world despite education campaigns and a cash injection of $151 million by the federal government last year.

The money, used to create the Australian Organ and Tissue Donation and Transplantation Authority, was supposed to boost dramatically the numbers of people willing to donate their organs, but little ground has been gained.

With 11.3 donors for every million people, Australia is among the least altruistic nations, well behind Spain with 34 donors each million, Portugal with 31 and the US with 24.

In Spain organ donation blossomed after the government set up a network of transplant coordinators in 139 intensive-care units across the country. Their job was to monitor emergency departments and tactfully discuss the donation process with the families of the dead. A survey found that of 200 families who declined to have their relatives' organs donated, 78 per cent changed their mind after the process was explained in detail.

But in Australia the waters are still murky. Many people who wish to donate have their decision overruled by family members after their death, leaving scores of patients lingering on waiting lists.

In 2008, 82 hearts were donated in Australia, but last year that dropped to 59—most from people who died from strokes. Another 41 people, including Tigano, missed out.

A quarter of those on the waiting list will die before a heart becomes available, usually within nine to 12 months. Another quarter need a mechanical pump to keep them alive while they wait for a transplant. The pumps cost up to $150,000 each, but once they are in place only about 5 per cent of the recipients die while waiting for a transplant.

Many people who wish to donate have their decision overruled by family members after their death, leaving scores of patients lingering on waiting lists.

Patients with heart failure usually fall into two camps. About 80 per cent have problems with their left ventricle, the main pumping chamber. In the rest, both ventricles have failed.

Up to 30 people a year with left ventricular problems are given pumps known as left ventricular assist devices, valued at about $100,000 each, which are paid for with money donated by benefactors. But it is money well spent, says a cardiothoracic surgeon, Paul Jansz, one of the doctors who gave Tigano his new heart.

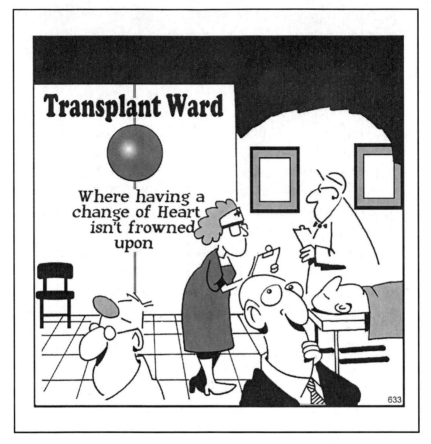

"Transplant ward—where having a change of heart isn't frowned upon," cartoon by Mark Lynch, www.CartoonStock.com. Copyright © Mark Lynch. Reproduction rights available from www.CartoonStock.com.

"Mechanical pumps are standard therapy in any transplant unit in the world now . . . and they're cost effective. If you don't have one you will either die or have multiple admissions to hospital, drugs and a temporary balloon pump," he said.

"Those in end-stage heart failure will do that up to four times a year, staying up to three weeks in hospital, which is a huge burden on the health dollar."

Most of those with the devices fitted also do better when they receive their donated heart because they have had time to put on weight and recover from their heart failure, Jansz said.

He met NSW health officials last week to explain that mechanical hearts were becoming so mainstream and clinically proven that the government needed to commit to funding heart transplant programs, as occurs in Victoria and South Australia.

"They were very receptive and accepting that this technology has come of age," Jansz said.

Tigano's artificial heart was also funded by benefactors, but if government funding was granted about 200 people a year could be helped.

Total artificial hearts are not new. The brand implanted in Tigano has been available overseas since 2004 and given to more than 850 patients worldwide. But it is not without its drawbacks. The maker, SynCardia, says about 70 per cent of 95 recipients studied developed an infection in their lungs, urinary tract or around the surgical site. Almost half suffered bleeding around the heart or lungs; about 17 per cent had problems with the implant malfunctioning; a third developed kidney dysfunction; and 10 per cent suffered a stroke.

But experts are quick to warn that only the "sickest of the sick" are given the heart in the first place—those who are expected to die within days or weeks. "Yes, there are complications and most of them are related to having a drive line into the skin or clots forming, but the alternative is far worse," says Jansz.

During his operation, Tigano's heart was removed before the artificial replacement was sewn into place, attached to the four main vessels, the aorta, vena cava and the pulmonary vein and artery.

Two plastic chambers take the place of the ventricles and can pump 9.5 litres of blood a minute.

The heart has only six moving parts and is driven by an external pneumatic pump, which is as big as a suitcase. The pump is portable and needs to be connected to a power supply but doctors think that within weeks Tigano can go home with a backpack version, giving him more quality of life as he awaits a donor.

Kuwait Is Determined to Improve Its Rate of Organ Donation

Habib Toumi

Habib Toumi is a reporter for the Gulf News, *an English-language newspaper published in Dubai. In the following viewpoint, he observes that Kuwait has made progress in its effort to raise awareness of the importance of organ donation, but it still has a long way to go to push up donation rates to those of Europe. Much of the challenge in addressing the resistance to organ donation in Kuwait is based on cultural and religious beliefs. Toumi contends that health officials believe that it is imperative to confront these misconceptions about organ donations not only to help patients who need organs, but also to alleviate the practice of organ trafficking.*

As you read, consider the following questions:

1. According to Dr. Mustafa Al-Mousawi, what percentage of Kuwaiti families give their consent to a loved one's organs after death?
2. What percentage of European families grant permission for organ donation, according to Dr. Al-Mousawi?

Habib Toumi, "Kuwait Expert Calls for Greater Organ Donation Awareness," *Gulf News*, October 17, 2011. Copyright © 2011 by Al Bawaba LTD. All rights reserved. Reproduced by permission.

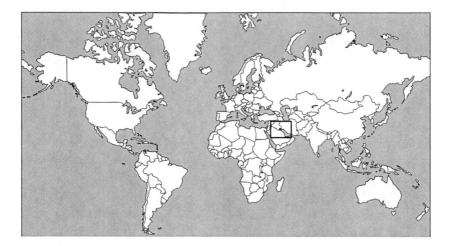

3. How did ancient religious leaders answer the question of whether it would be permissible to remove a valuable jewel from the stomach of a deceased person?

A health official in Kuwait said that the country had moved forward in organ donation awareness, but insisted that more was needed.

"Kuwait has relatively high rates of organ donation when compared with other Middle Eastern countries," Dr Mustafa Al-Mousawi, the head of the Ministry of Health's (MoH) organ procurement unit, said.

"However, it is still behind the US and Europe in this area. We have a slightly higher rate in Kuwait because we have been organizing ourselves since 1996. We started a course, with the help of Eurotransplant [a nonprofit organization that acts as mediator between organ donor and recipient], which made a great deal of difference, but there's still a lot of work to be done," he said, quoted by *Kuwait Times* on Monday [October 2011].

Twenty-Five Per Cent of Deceased Donate

Around 25 per cent of the families of deceased individuals in Kuwait give their consent when contacted to donate their loved ones' organs to save others' lives.

"While this is a higher-than-average figure for the Middle East, however, it's still some way behind the same figure in Europe, which currently stands at 75 per cent, so there's still progress to be made in this area," Al-Mousawi said.

The senior MoH official attributed the differing attitudes towards organ donation between the Middle East and Europe to culture.

"Many from Islamic backgrounds feel that it is wrong to alter the body of the deceased. However, we asked religious leaders about this issue specifically and they said that because you are saving people's lives as a result, it is permissible. There is a verse in the Quran that says that saving one person's life is like saving a whole nation," he said.

The issue of the acceptability of altering or performing any form of surgery on a deceased person's body is an age-old one, he said.

Religious Leaders

"Religious leaders, many centuries ago, asked this same question. For example they asked if it would be permissible to remove a valuable jewel from the stomach of the deceased. They decided that it would be acceptable if the jewel was the property of another."

Another question was about removing a living baby from its mother's womb if the mother has passed away before giving birth.

"Would it not be acceptable to operate on the body of the deceased, in order to save the life of another person?"

However, a survey . . . highlighted how culture influences people's attitudes towards the issue.

"It Is Not Right"

"It is not right. We should leave like we came," Aysha, a 56-year-old mother of four, said. "However, if one of my sons was in need of an organ I would hope that he would receive one from someone who had been a donor. Maybe it is something we judge from afar without thinking about the further consequences."

Sara, a 22-year-old Kuwaiti student, insisted, however, that it was not culture that prevented people from donating or approving the donation of organs, but something far more basic and self-centered.

According to Dr Mustafa Al-Mousawi [of Kuwait's Ministry of Health], organ donation would certainly reduce waiting lists for organs, but would also eradicate many disturbing practices that some people awaiting transplants adopt out of desperation.

"Many just do not like the idea of it," she said. "It bothers them, and they do not want to consider why it is important and what a difference it would make. I think it is selfish to refuse. Saving a life is one of the best things we can do as humans, even if it is something 'we do' in death."

According to Dr Al-Mousawi, organ donation would certainly reduce waiting lists for organs, but would also eradicate many disturbing practices that some people awaiting transplants adopt out of desperation.

He said that many people from the Middle East travelled to poor areas in India, Pakistan, the Philippines and Egypt in search of organs for sale, despite the legal and ethical questions such behavior raises.

Unrelated Donors

In the past, there have also been numerous instances in Kuwait of unrelated donors suddenly offering a kidney to a "friend" awaiting a transplant. . . . Upon further investigation, however, the donor was often discovered to be selling the organ in question to the other individual and to have no other relationship to them.

Dr Al-Mousawi added, however, that this problem was successfully combated with further regulation and mandatory scrutiny of any case in which an unrelated donor comes forward to announce a wish to donate.

England's Minority Communities Have a Low Rate of Organ Donations

Ben Whitelaw

Ben Whitelaw is a reporter for the Guardian. *In the following viewpoint, he claims that the low rate of organ donation within minority communities in England has become a serious public health issue. To address the crisis, health organizations have implemented programs to raise awareness of the problem and deal with cultural and religious misconceptions that prevent people from registering as donors. Whitelaw reports that health officials have found it more effective to go into communities and utilize existing social networks to get the message out to minority groups.*

As you read, consider the following questions:

1. According to the British National Health Service, what percentage of people waiting for an organ transplant are from BME (black and minority ethnic) communities?

2. How many people from BME groups does Whitelaw say were signed to the organ donation register from 2009–2011 through the Peer Educator program?

Ben Whitelaw, "Transplanting a Culture of Organ Donations," *The Guardian*, July 12, 2011. Copyright © 2011 by The Guardian. All rights reserved. Reproduced by permission.

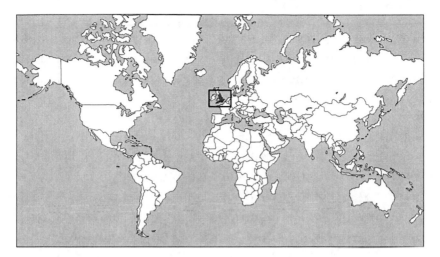

3. What did a fatwa issued in late 1990s say about organ donations, according to officials?

Black and minority ethnic groups are under-represented on the organ donation register, but face-to-face events can help.

Organ donation within BME (black and minority ethnic) communities is becoming a serious public health issue, as the need for transplants among its members increases. According to NHS Blood and Transplant, 26% of people waiting for an organ transplant are from BME groups, with the majority of those needing a kidney transplant.

However, in March just 0.4% of those on the organ donor register were black and 1.3% were from Asian ethnic groups. With the success of organ transplantation heavily dependent on blood type and with very few type B donors—the predominant blood type of Asian and Afro-Caribbean groups—on the register, the racial mix of donors needs to match demand more closely.

In a recent paper, Gurch Randhawa, professor of diversity in public health and director at the institute of health at the University of Bedfordshire, found that minority ethnic groups are disproportionately affected by demand for transplants compared to the white population as a result of genetic predisposition and increased prevalence of underlying conditions.

His research, published last week by the Race Equality Foundation to coincide with National Transplant Week, also concluded that those in the BME community were prevented from joining the register due to religious and cultural factors that meant they did not think they were permitted to donate. Common fears included thinking that cremation would be delayed and that doctors wouldn't work as hard to cure an illness for someone registered for organ donation.

"Much like other countries which are far more successful than us, we've got to find a way of proactively addressing these concerns with the public," says Dr Randhawa.

Common fears [about organ donation] included thinking that cremation would be delayed and that doctors wouldn't work as hard to cure an illness for someone registered for organ donation.

He says the key is making sure that people in BME groups are fully informed. That doesn't mean throwing leaflets and DVDs at them either, he says, but speaking to people face-to-face. Funded by the Department of Health as part of the organ donation task force delivery board, Randhawa has attended events around the country and recently joined religious gatherings in Neasden and Chigwell to talk to Hindu and Sikh communities.

"Where it works best is when you've got the community on their terms in their environment," he says. "If they then want to get faith-based advice, it's far better that those people are in the room when you're giving them that information so that they can be part of the dialogue."

Religious Objections

This grassroots approach to organ donation has worked elsewhere: In July 2009, Kidney Research UK instigated the Peer

Educator programme to raise awareness about all aspects of organ donation, particularly the issue of consent to using organs following death, which is more frequently withheld by people in BME groups.

The programme enlisted seven peer educators from Harrow in London to conduct awareness-raising sessions about organ donation. Over a two-year period, they went out to mela festivals, libraries and places of worship, signing up more than 2,000 people to the organ donation register.

Neerja Jain, a projects development manager at Kidney Research UK, says: "Sometimes concerns were of a religious nature, but some were they were just concerns that Joe Bloggs walking along the street might have. Sometimes it was people who were very open minded but perhaps had never thought about it and never given the opportunity to talk about it."

"Some people didn't want to approach the stall and some events didn't want to have people in," adds Tim Hoyle, public health projects officer for NHS Harrow and health trainer lead on the project. "But then as word of mouth got round and people heard about it, they began to embrace it. What would often happen is that people might not approach the stall the first time, but might do on the second or third. It was a drip feed effect."

In one particular case, having found it difficult to get those from the Muslim population to sign up, a peer educator contacted the Islamic Sharia Council for guidance and discovered that a fatwa was issued in the late 1990s saying organ donation was allowed and seen as a positive step.

"One time a Muslim woman came to one of the stalls and said 'I'm not allowed to do it,'" says Hoyle. "Our peer educator gave her the fatwa, she went away, read it and came back and signed up on the spot. That was the barrier for her. It's just about letting people find a way for themselves."

"I really do think this sort of grassroots approach has a tremendous amount of applicability across a wide range of healthcare," says Prof Anthony Warrens, dean for education at Barts and the London School of Medicine and Dentistry, who witnessed the prevalence of kidney disease in his former clinical practice in west London and was subsequently supported by Kidney Research UK to undertake research that culminated in the Peer Educator programme. "If you compare the cost of a programme like this with the cost of treating a patient, irrespective of the human benefit of helping that person, the cost to the NHS is an easy one to justify. Our model has been shown to work."

Money for the Peer Educator programme has run out, with new funding being sought to continue the scheme in other areas. "All the evidence shows you, if you want organ donation to become usual you have to make it accessible in everybody's day-to-day lives," says Dr Randhawa. "You've got to think about the ways of getting people to talk about it and the only way to do that is to do it via their normal social network."

Ontario Has Wide Variations in Organ Donation Rates

Megan Ogilvie and Patrick Cain

Megan Ogilvie and Patrick Cain are staff reporters for the Toronto Star. In the following viewpoint, they examine the stark differences in organ donation registration rates throughout the Canadian province of Ontario. Ogilvie and Cain report that smaller cities such as Sudbury and swaths of the North Bay region have high rates of registration, while the largest city, Toronto, has the lowest. Health officials blame a variety of factors, including cultural differences and the registration process itself, for the variation. They plan to offer online registration for organ donation and raise awareness in minority communities through outreach and education, the authors conclude.

As you read, consider the following questions:

1. According to the viewpoint, what is the rate of organ donor registration in Sudbury, Ontario?
2. What do the authors say is the provincial rate of organ donor registration?
3. What percentage of Ontarians say they support organ donation, according to the Trillium Gift of Life Network?

Megan Ogilvie and Patrick Cain, "Are We Less Caring? Toronto Last in Organ Donors List," *The Toronto Star*, April 24, 2010. Copyright © 2010 by Torstar Syndication Services. All rights reserved. Reproduced by permission.

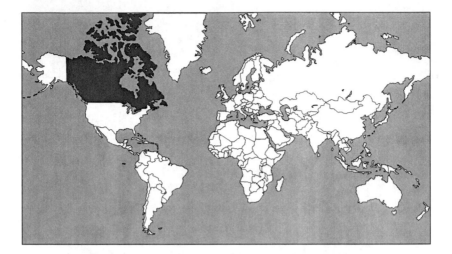

On the outskirts of Sudbury, on each of the two roads that lead into town, you will see a large red billboard emblazoned with a simple message: "Be an organ donor. Tell your family."

These unique billboards have remained in the same spot for 10 years. A constant reminder to all who go to Sudbury that organ donation can save lives.

"It's only seven words," says Betty O'Reilly, whose family erected the signs after the death of her son, Michael, in 1999. "That's so you can read it very quickly while you're driving."

Betty and her husband, Mel, watched helplessly as Michael, who had cystic fibrosis, died at the age of 37 while waiting for a double lung transplant. They were shocked that no lungs became available during the 13-month wait.

The O'Reillys have spent the last decade raising awareness for organ donation, heading up their cause from the Irish Heritage Club of Sudbury. They have issued stickers and reusable grocery bags printed with their message, and each year they organize a walk to inspire community members to become organ donors.

Their efforts seem to be working.

Raising Awareness

According to an analysis by the *Star*, Sudbury has the second highest rate of organ donor registration in the province. About 34 per cent of residents have registered their consent for organ and tissue donation with Ontario's Trillium Gift of Life Network.

Betty does not think their persistence and simple message would have broken through in Toronto.

"It's easier to spread the word in a smaller city," she says. "We really feel that our efforts have shown an increase in donation."

That it is easier to effect change in smaller communities, where people are more likely to connect with a friend of a friend of a friend, is likely just one of the reasons there is wide variation in organ donor registration rates in Ontario.

Variations in Organ Donation Rates in Ontario

Data obtained by the *Star*, released by Ontario's Ministry of Health under access-to-information laws, shows a stark difference in rates of organ donor registration.

Swaths of northeastern Ontario from Muskoka through to Sudbury and North Bay and the northern shore of Lake Superior have registration rates over 30 per cent. A neighbourhood in the north part of North Bay has the highest rate in Ontario at 43 per cent.

In Hamilton, 25 per cent of residents have signed the donor registry, while 20 per cent of residents in London and 15 per cent of residents in Ottawa have registered. The provincial average is 17 per cent.

Toronto sits at the bottom of the list. Only four per cent of residents who live in neighbourhoods in the northwest of the city register to be organ donors and rates in many other enclaves hover around eight per cent.

The Importance of Organ Donation in Ontario

People are often surprised to learn how rare it is for someone to become an organ donor. For an individual to become an organ donor, they must die in hospital while on life support, which accounts for only a small percentage of deaths. (This is not the case for tissue donation, which can take place in most cases when someone has died, as long as the tissue is suitable for transplantation.)

Because the opportunities for organ donation are relatively rare and the impact is lifesaving, it's important that Ontarians give serious thought to organ and tissue donation and register their consent to donate. This way you can ensure that your donation decision, if and when needed, is made known to your family. Also, by registering your consent to donate, you relieve your family of the burden of making this decision on your behalf.

"Organ & Tissue Donation,"
BeADonor.ca, 2008. Copyright © 2008 by Gift of Life.
All rights reserved. Reproduced by permission.

Reasons for the Variations

It's not surprising there is variation across Ontario's sprawling 1 million square kilometres. But why does Toronto have the lowest rates? Are those approximately 800,000 Ontarians who live north of Sudbury more generous than the 12 million who live in the south?

There are no definitive answers without study. Experts say the variation is likely due to a confluence of factors, including the small-town effect, an overly cumbersome registration process for Ontarians who still have the red-and-white health card, and even the average age of a city's residents.

North Bay, which has the highest organ donor registration rate in the province, is made up of residents in older age brackets, which may impact the community's high rate, says Tiziana Silveri, vice-president of surgery at North Bay General Hospital.

In a diverse city like Toronto there will be dozens of different interpretations of death, which means not everyone will agree to donating their organs.

Cultural Differences

Cultural differences may also play a role. Organ donation generally resonates strongly with people of Western origin and descent, says Kerry Bowman, a bioethicist at the University of Toronto's Joint Centre for Bioethics. In a diverse city like Toronto there will be dozens of different interpretations of death, which means not everyone will agree to donating their organs.

"For a lot of people, brain death is not an accepted form or definition of death," Bowman says, noting he himself is a proponent of organ donation. "And it's not just about education. There are deeper cultural reasons that need to be respected."

Versha Prakash, vice-president of operations at the Trillium Gift of Life Network, says it's important for the organization to understand why 90 per cent of Ontarians say they support organ donation, yet only 17 per cent have registered their intent to donate. The regional variation seen in Ontario, where rural communities are more likely to have higher registration rates, mirror patterns in other jurisdictions, including many American states, she says.

Confronting the Crisis

Trillium is working to make more people aware of the registration process. Prakash says the organization is preparing information packages to include in the 1.4 million health card renewal applications that are sent out annually. And, she adds, Trillium is working with the province to implement online registration.

Awareness efforts focused in the GTA [greater Toronto area] include working with faith leaders to dispel common misconceptions about organ donation, Prakash says. In 2009, Trillium, in partnership with Catholic, Jewish and Muslim faith leaders, produced education brochures to show how organ donation is consistent with those faith beliefs.

This year [2010], Trillium will reach out to leaders in Toronto's different ethnic communities, including secular leaders in the Chinese and South Asian communities, to discuss the importance of organ donation.

"We hope to engage secular leaders . . . to help spread that message," Prakash says. "We need to attack this on multiple fronts."

A Soldier's Death Gives Life to Another Man

Meg Jones

Meg Jones is a reporter for the Milwaukee Journal Sentinel. *In the following viewpoint, she chronicles the story of an American soldier, Private Steven Drees, who was mortally injured in Afghanistan, shipped to Landstuhl Regional Medical Center in Germany, and upon his death had his liver donated to a German man. Jones reports that many American soldiers who die at Landstuhl have agreed to donate their organs, which have greatly benefited a number of German citizens waiting for transplants. Jones explains that Germany has had a historically low rate of organ donor registration that can be attributed to the legacy of Nazi experiments during World War II and a reaction to the totalitarian political system in East Germany during the Cold War.*

As you read, consider the following questions:

1. According to Jones, what percentage of German adults registered to become organ donors?
2. According to the Deutsche Stiftung Organtransplantation, how many American military members who died at Landstuhl donated organs for transplantation between 2005 to 2010?

Meg Jones, "A Soldier's Death Gives Life to Another Man," Pulitzer Center on Crisis Reporting, April 23, 2011. Reproduced by permission.

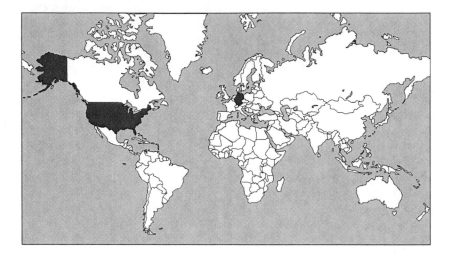

3. How many people does Jones say are on organ donation waiting lists in Germany?

Hot shell casings cartwheeled around Pvt. Steven Drees as he stood in the gunner's turret firing hundreds of rounds from his M240 machine gun.

It was a sunny June afternoon in Afghanistan's Korengal Valley, and Drees had just grabbed his fifth box of ammunition from the platoon medic when he was hit.

With bullets raining down like hail on the armored vehicle filled with American soldiers, a single bullet clipped the edge of the turret before smashing into Drees' right cheek, taking out his right eye and pushing through his brain.

Medic Luke Spangler caught the Wisconsin teenager as he fell into the vehicle, quickly checked his injuries and worked feverishly to stop the bleeding. He cradled Drees as the vehicle raced to an aid station.

It was the first stop of a final journey that would end four days later in Germany.

As his mother, father and twin brother traveled from Peshtigo to say goodbye, somewhere in Europe—most likely elsewhere in Germany—a 62-year-old man was about to receive a life-changing organ donation.

The man would never know Drees' name, and Drees' family would never know his identity. But the two men will forever be linked by a sniper's bullet and the selfless act of a soldier killed less than a month after leaving for Afghanistan on his 19th birthday.

It's a rarely told fact of the wars in Iraq and Afghanistan that a significant number of U.S. service members who die at the large American military hospital in Germany are donating their organs to whoever needs them. And the people who need them are Germans.

Like every U.S. military member deploying to Afghanistan and Iraq, Drees was asked if he wished to be an organ donor.

He said yes.

Drees had debated the merits of organ donation in an ethics class at Peshtigo High School, and his family knew his wishes.

After being wounded, Drees was evacuated to Landstuhl Regional Medical Center in Germany. Donated organs must be transplanted within hours, so his liver was given to someone on a waiting list in the Eurotransplant system, which serves seven countries, including Germany. Although transport to another country is possible, it most likely stayed in Germany.

It's a rarely told fact of the wars in Iraq and Afghanistan that a significant number of U.S. service members who die at the large American military hospital in Germany are donating their organs to whoever needs them. And the people who need them are Germans.

Germany has one of the lowest organ donation participation rates in the Eurotransplant system. There are hundreds more organ transplants in Germany every year than are actually donated by Germans.

Attitudes toward organ donation in Germany are shaped by Nazi medical experiments in World War II as well as the legacy of the East German health care system under socialism, in which people had no control over the fate of their bodies.

As a result:

- In Germany, 17% of adults are registered to become organ donors. In contrast, the figure in America is 37% and in Wisconsin, it's 54%. Among the U.S. military, the percentages are even higher since everyone deploying to a combat zone is asked about organ donation wishes.

- Landstuhl, the largest U.S. military hospital outside America, is one of the top hospitals for organ donations in its region in Germany, even though it has relatively few beds.

- Roughly half of the troops who died at Landstuhl from combat injuries since 2005 were organ donors. That's the first year the U.S. military allowed organs to be donated by American troops who died in Germany from wounds suffered in Iraq or Afghanistan.

- From 2005 through 2010, 34 American military members who died at Landstuhl donated a total of 142 organs, according to Deutsche Stiftung Organtransplantation, the German organ organization known as DSO. Last year 10 of the 12 service members who died at Landstuhl were donors, giving 45 organs. In 2009, the year Drees died, five of the 12 Americans who died at Landstuhl donated a total of 17 organs.

More than 30 patients on waiting lists were saved last year by organs donated by U.S. military members at Landstuhl, said Undine Samuel, a physician and medical director of the DSO region that includes Landstuhl.

"That's a great amount," said Samuel. "I'd like to explain better to Germans so they know the part Americans are doing here. I'd like to say thanks."

Attitudes toward organ donation in Germany are shaped by Nazi medical experiments in World War II as well as the legacy of the East German health care system under socialism, in which people had no control over the fate of their bodies.

Influenced by History

In Germany, decisions over whether to use the bodies of some for the benefit of others are laden with historical and emotional baggage stemming from racial laws during World War II and vast differences in organ donation policies in East and West Germany in the decades before the Berlin Wall fell in 1989.

Outrage over Nazi atrocities led to the Helsinki human rights accords and international bioethics rules. Germany went a step further; the first two articles in its postwar constitution deal with individuals' rights of bodily integrity. Decades later, after the reunification of East and West Germany in the 1990s, Germans would pack town hall meetings to vigorously debate the issue of who has the right to determine when someone is dead and how their body will be used.

"In the United States, organ transplantation organizations have popularized the motto 'Donate your organs so that others might live.' That motto, however, has a completely different meaning in postwar Germany," wrote University of Wisconsin assistant professor Linda Hogle, a medical anthropologist who studied German organ procurement policies in the 1990s and published a book on the subject.

In West Germany where memories of the Holocaust made the notion of protecting bodily integrity paramount, "physicians wouldn't even approach a family about possibly donating organs because they were so afraid the family might be disturbed or it might upset them," Hogle said in an interview in her Madison office.

Opinions were just as emotional in socialist East Germany—but for different reasons. People injured in an accident might be taken to a major medical center, and if they died, any body part or tissue could be used for experiments, research or organ donations.

"If you want to call it presumed consent, it was like an extreme form of presumed consent. There was no possibility of even saying 'I do not want my organs to be used.' It was just going to happen," Hogle said.

Clouding the issue further is that Germany has a vibrant, cutting-edge medical system that makes it a leading country within Europe for organ transplant technology.

East German medical centers performed far fewer transplants than the more technologically advanced hospitals in the West—mostly kidneys. The perception was that Communist Party members got preference, and the country drew donors from a small pool of neighboring socialist countries. Consequently, many East Germans spent years on waiting lists.

When the two nations reunified in the early 1990s, there was some resentment over how to serve the needs of the former East Germany while still keeping some sense of fairness and balance with donors and recipients from West Germany and other European nations.

To this day, Germans are caught in what Hogle calls a "damned if you do, damned if you don't" struggle: Push for more donations, and they raise the specter of Nazi medical policies; back off, and they risk the appearance that they're poaching organs from other countries. Clouding the issue further is that Germany has a vibrant, cutting-edge medical system that makes it a leading country within Europe for organ transplant technology.

Even though Germany lags in actual donations, being perceived as practicing good medicine—through organ transplants—is a means of contrition.

Anonymity Is Strict

For Steven Drees' family and friends, German attitudes toward organ donation made no difference. Like many grieving families who give consent for organ donation by their loved ones, all they cared about was that his liver was given to someone who needed it, that something good come from something tragic.

Though some organ recipients in the U.S. meet their donors or donors' families, German law is strict about anonymity. The age and gender of organ recipients and donors are released, and recipients can send anonymous thank you notes to donor families through German organ officials.

Even though Germany lags in actual donations, being perceived as practicing good medicine—through organ transplants—is a means of contrition.

Drees' family received a letter telling them a 62-year-old man was given his liver. The soldier's parents and girlfriend wish they could learn more about the man.

"I'd like to know their circumstances and to know what is going on with them, to know they had loved ones, to know they aren't alone," said his girlfriend, Stacia Baker.

Drees was close to his maternal grandfather, a Navy veteran who died of leukemia when Steven was a youngster.

"The thing that settles me the most," said his mother, Dawn Bayer, "is that at 62 years old, I know he's probably someone's grandpa. So Steven saved someone's grandpa."

Filled with Energy

If the man who received Drees' liver in late June 2009 could find out more about his donor, this is what he would learn:

Before he became a soldier, before he became an organ donor, Steven Drees was a bundle of energy who seemed to speed from one activity to the next, collecting friends along the way. When he was 7 or 8 he told his dad he wanted to be a baseball pitcher, so Paul Drees bought him a glove and ball and the two spent hours in the backyard practicing.

Steven played video games and basketball and had a winning smile. He liked fast cars, and he wasn't embarrassed to hug and kiss his mother in front of his basketball teammates, his coaches remembered. He wanted to be a gym teacher.

Though he was a twin, he and his brother Chuck looked nothing alike. The boys were close growing up but had different hobbies. Their high school graduation photos illustrate the difference—Chuck is pictured with his truck; Steven with his basketball jerseys. Steven was born seconds before Chuck—it was a C-section—a fact he never let Chuck forget. Their parents later divorced, each staying in Peshtigo and remaining close to their boys. Steven joined the Army before he graduated in May 2008 from Peshtigo High School, and left for boot camp a few weeks after commencement.

Four months before he shipped out to Afghanistan, on his last visit home to Peshtigo, Drees had a long conversation with his mother. He went over all the details of his funeral and burial if something happened. It was unusual for him because he wasn't a details type of guy.

"I was crying and he kept saying 'Mom, I need to tell you this stuff,'" Bayer said.

He wanted to be buried next to his grandfather in the pretty cemetery overlooking the Peshtigo River. He also didn't want anyone to cry at his funeral.

When his parents and brother visited him in Fort Carson, Colo., before he deployed, he played them a song by the band

Everlast called "Letters Home from the Garden of Stone" which include the lyrics "'Cause I don't know the man who kills me, and I don't know these men I kill." He gave his father a CD of the music.

"Steven said, 'You need to listen to this,'" said Paul Drees. "I guess it was easier for him to play the song than to have him explain it to us, because he knew what he was getting into."

In the weeks and months after his son's death, Paul Drees listened to the song often, finding solace in the words.

Expecting Trouble

Drees shipped out from Fort Carson, home base of the Army's 4th Infantry Division, on May 26, 2009. It was his 19th birthday. His unit—Delta Co., 2nd Battalion, 12th Infantry Regiment—arrived in Afghanistan two days later.

Spc. Luke Spangler, an Ohio native, remembered Drees as someone in tune with himself, a good soldier who most likely would have been the next in his platoon to get promoted. Though a gun turret can be a scary, intense place, Drees managed to boost the morale of his platoon and keep things light. One of his Army buddies snapped a photo of Drees on base, wearing bunny ears and a large grin.

Reflecting a level of trust that's difficult to understand for anyone who has never been in combat, Spangler said Drees was the one man he wanted watching his back.

Spangler, 30, knew Drees had signed up to be an organ donor since he and the rest of their close-knit unit had talked about organ donations.

"Being an organ donor was way more personal for us as a platoon. Steven was very conscious about his decision to be an organ donor—that if he couldn't save his life he wanted to save someone else's life," Spangler said.

On June 24, Drees and his platoon were sent out on a route clearance mission after receiving word about an impro-

Landstuhl Regional Medical Center

The Landstuhl Regional Medical Center [LRMC] is the largest American hospital outside the United States and is located in the German state of Rheinland-Pfalz, 11 kilometers west of Kaiserslautern and five kilometers south of Ramstein Air Base. . . .

Today, LRMC provides primary and tertiary (specialized) care, hospitalization, and medical treatment for more than 52,000 local American military personnel and their families. It also provides specialized care for the more than 250,000 additional American military personnel and their families in the European Theater.

The staff of the hospital is made up of 50 percent Army, 15 percent Air Force and 35 percent civilian personnel. The hospital has more than 110 physicians, 250 nurses, 40 Medical Service Corps officers, 900 enlisted personnel and 550 civilian employees. And the Landstuhl military community is the only Army medical facility to house an Air Force aeromedical evacuation unit.

Landstuhl served as the primary medical treatment center for injuries during Operations Desert Shield and Storm, but the facility has also treated nonmilitary personnel injuries. It was the treatment point for hundreds of Bosnian refugees injured in the 1994 Sarajevo marketplace bombing, and it treated American and Kenyan victims of the 1998 U.S. embassy bombing in Nairobi.

Today, LRMC provides medical treatment to those injured during Operation Enduring Freedom in Afghanistan and Operation Iraqi Freedom, and is a fixed medical facility assisting in the Balkan operations.

"Landstuhl Regional Medical Center,"
GoArmy.com, 2012.

vised explosive device nearby. Several armored vehicles pulled out of a Forward Operating Base in Asadabad traveling east and took some enemy fire on the way out. The soldiers were expecting trouble on the return trip that afternoon.

As the platoon's medic, Spangler always rode in the last truck in the convoy along with the platoon sergeant. Drees was their gunner. Before the mission, Drees' main weapon, an MK19 grenade launcher, was not working so he brought an M240 machine gun.

On the way back, the unit was ambushed, taking heavy fire from at least four positions.

With the other MRAP armored vehicles about 300 to 600 feet ahead on the roadway, Drees' vehicle drove off the road about 300 feet toward the heavy fire. Drees was firing his weapon full blast, shooting more than 500 rounds, Spangler said. Bullets struck the MRAP's radiator, gas tank and engine. Spangler had just handed up a fresh box of ammunition to Drees when the gunner was hit in the face.

"He tried to stay up; he was fighting when he went down. When I caught him he was localizing pain, trying to grab for his face. He was somewhat coherent but he had lost his right eye. I got the head wound bleeding to stop. I got him back to the aid station—that took about 15 minutes. We were able to hook him up to saline, get his airway open. . . . I was breathing for him on the bag for a while."

It took about 45 minutes for a medical helicopter to arrive at the aid station. The chopper took Drees to Bagram Airfield, where he received more treatment. Then he was flown to Landstuhl.

"Steven was probably one of my worst casualties up to that point, and I still had hope even when I left him on the bird. I worked like hell to get him out of there," Spangler said. "Even if there was a 5% chance he would make it, I was praying for that."

Though the military sends casualty notification officers to the homes of fallen service members, families of the wounded are notified by phone. Within hours of the ambush, Bayer received a phone call from someone at Fort Carson.

Information was sketchy at first, but she and her ex-husband, Paul Drees, were told death could be imminent. Long hours passed before they were told he was stabilized and on his way to Germany.

His twin sent out a Twitter message to their friends in Peshtigo. It said simply that Steven had been shot in the head in Afghanistan, and asked everyone to pray.

Lea Beier, who had known the Drees twins since third grade, was at home when she got the tweet.

"It was really short. We were like—what?" Beier said. She went on Facebook to learn more, and then organized a vigil that night at the baseball diamond on the outskirts of Peshtigo, the same field where Drees had played baseball. About 100 people showed up, including most of the 2008 graduation class.

"I thought there's no way he's going to die. He'll come back to us," Beier said.

A few nights later, she organized another vigil at the same spot. This time most of the community turned out. Beier bought all of the small candles at the local Dollar Tree store, and arranged them in Drees' initials on the baseball diamond. They read poems and shared words of support and comfort. By then, Beier recalled, they were praying for a miracle.

Family Grants Permission

Each family of the mortally wounded is offered a U.S. government-paid trip to Germany to say goodbye to their loved one at Landstuhl; not all accept, but many, like the Drees family, do. If the patient is a potential organ donor, the family is asked for permission.

Under the military's European Regional Medical Command guidelines, next of kin must OK the donor's wishes before organs can be taken in Germany even if, like Drees, a signed organ donor card already exists. If the family objects, organs are not removed. That differs from America, where most states—including Wisconsin—do not require consent from next of kin if the organ donor has made their wishes known.

Insel Angus, a registered nurse who is Landstuhl's liaison to the German organ procurement organization, could think of only one family that refused to donate a loved one's organs because they wouldn't be going to American recipients. All families are told that because of time limits, organs cannot be transported back to the United States.

As Drees' family flew to Germany, their minds were in different places. Paul Drees had come to grips with the fact that he was flying to Landstuhl to say goodbye. Dawn Bayer still held out hope.

At Landstuhl, doctors told them the grim prognosis. Drees was hooked up to machines, and a bandage covered the right side of his head. But otherwise, he looked like he should have been able to sit up and get out of his hospital bed. They were told he would never recover, that his brain was dead. They signed organ donation papers. His heart, liver and kidneys were viable.

Chuck Drees told doctors that his brother's heart was too big for anyone else to use and he wanted it to stay with his twin. The other organs could be donated.

The family's signatures set in motion a complex process starting with notification of Germany's organ procurement organization. Waiting lists were scrutinized through a computer database and hospitals notified. Before organs are removed, transplant recipients must be identified and transplant teams ready.

By the time this was done, Drees' body was starting to shut down and his kidneys were no longer viable. To Drees' family it seemed to take forever; at one point, they considered withdrawing their approval. But eventually a potential liver recipient was located.

Each family member went in alone to say goodbye. They were allowed as much time as they wished.

"I just held him and gave him a kiss and told him I love him," said Paul Drees.

Chaplain Joseph Sheldon, a Navy commander and Episcopalian minister, gives spiritual comfort to the families that come to Landstuhl to say farewell. Often a final prayer and short bedside ceremony is held in Landstuhl's intensive care unit with chaplains such as Sheldon holding the hands of family members to help them let go of someone so full of life and promise.

The decisions by the American military families have a profound effect in Germany.

"We're thanking God for the life of the soldier or Marine, letting them know that everyone who loves them is with them, we don't want them to go but we're giving them permission to go and we're asking God to give new life to the person who will get the organs," said Sheldon.

Americans' Outsized Impact

The decisions by the American military families have a profound effect in Germany. In 2010, only six out of 205 hospitals in the DSO's central region, which includes the large cities of Frankfurt and Mainz, had more organ donors than Landstuhl, and four of those six were university hospitals with thousands of beds. Landstuhl has 150.

Further, few patients die at Landstuhl because the critically wounded are first sent to medical facilities in Afghanistan and

Iraq. For those who make it to Landstuhl, the main funnel point for wounded traveling back to the U.S., the average stay is only 72 hours.

Of the 15,000-plus combat casualty patients admitted to Landstuhl over the last decade, 93 have died at the hospital through Dec. 31, 2010, a 0.62% mortality rate.

American troops who die at Landstuhl—where the average age of combat casualties is 27—are ideal organ donors because they're young, fit and healthy. In contrast, almost one third of Germans who donate organs are 65 or older. The best candidates are those, like Drees, who suffer a catastrophic head wound, which allows the body to continue to circulate blood and oxygen through organs, and those who lose limbs and suffer blood loss that ultimately result in death, but not enough blood loss to affect organs, said Lt. Col. Stewart Mc-Carver, an Army surgeon at Landstuhl.

Teams of German doctors and technicians come to Landstuhl to remove the organs; American military doctors do not assist in the retrieval. A different team handles each organ; if several organs are being donated, dozens of medical personnel are involved.

Since livers typically last 10 to 12 hours after removal, it's likely Drees' organ went to a hospital within a five-hour travel radius, such as Hannover or Berlin, leaving enough time for the transplant operation, said Jens Von Schlichting, a deceased-donor coordinator for DSO.

In Germany, 12,000 people are on waiting lists and three to four die daily. The average wait in Germany for a heart or liver is six to 12 months; the wait for a kidney is six years. One in five people waiting for a liver in Germany dies before one becomes available.

Some like Susanne Lang, 46, have to leave Germany to live. Lang was born with cystic fibrosis and waited so long for a double lung transplant she was advised to leave her home near Frankfurt and go to Austria, where she got the organs that saved her life.

Others like Allan Sandlin are lucky. The Episcopalian priest was a church rector in Frankfurt when he became very sick from bile duct disease two years after moving to Germany from America. In 2002, a year after going on the list, the American received a liver from a 21-year-old who suffered a brain aneurysm in Austria.

Sandlin, now 58 and working at a church in Decatur, Ga., said his nationality played no factor in German doctors placing him on the list in Germany. And because he was living and working in Germany at the time he needed a liver, the entire expense—medications, hospitalization, rehabilitation, even mileage to drive to the rehab center—was paid by the German government.

If Drees' family could meet the man who received his liver, it might be someone like Hans-Peter Wohn—a 63-year-old retired house painter from Wiesbaden who received a liver in 1992 from a 46-year-old woman who died of a cerebral hemorrhage.

To honor her memory, Wohn has worked with an organ transplant group in Germany, consulting with organ recipients and speaking to schools and civic groups to break through the taboos of organ donation. His work is part of a broader national campaign. The DSO has tried billboards, TV and radio advertising, organ donation endorsements by famous German athletes, presentations to groups, promotional pamphlets, and heart-shaped pins with the slogan "For Life, For Organ Transplants" in German.

Wohn was unaware of the significant number of organs donated at Landstuhl by American military members.

"Most recipients don't know if it's German, American, Russian, black, white, young, old—the only thing they know is, does the organ work?" said Wohn as he sipped coffee in a restaurant in Wiesbaden. "It's not a matter of how Americans or Germans deal with organ donation, it's how humanity does."

"My Heart Hurts"

Days before Drees deployed, his girlfriend suspected she was pregnant but wasn't certain. By the time she knew for sure, Drees was in Afghanistan. She e-mailed him the news.

Drees told his Army buddies he was going to be a dad. He was excited about settling down with his family when he returned home.

Because Baker and Drees were not married—they had decided to wait and consider marriage when he returned from Afghanistan—she didn't get a call from the military when he was wounded. It was Steven's mother who called her with the initial news, and then called from Germany after he died.

About a month and a half after Steven's death, an ultrasound showed the baby was a boy.

Spangler contacted Drees' family when he returned to Fort Carson, and they asked him to look in on Baker, who also lived in Colorado. When it came time for her baby's birth in February 2010, Baker knew she wanted a man close to Drees to be with her. Drees' brother Chuck couldn't make it out to Colorado, so she asked Spangler to be there.

He stayed by her side throughout labor, holding Baker's hand, coaching her through the pain. When her son was born, it was Spangler who cut the umbilical cord.

"He was the one person who saved Steven long enough to get him to Germany so his family could say goodbye," said Baker. "It was amazing not only for me and for Steven's family but for Luke to cut little Steven into the world."

For Spangler, who would lose his squad leader in an IED blast a few weeks after Drees was killed, as well as several more soldiers from his battalion, watching the birth of his buddy's baby was almost too much to bear.

"It was a real emotional time. I was still dealing with the trauma of Steven's death and seeing his child that looked so much like him and standing there with the smells of blood and childbirth, it was almost surreal," said Spangler.

"I was honored, of course. The little guy squirted me right in the face—they said that was Steven all the way."

Baker has since become very close to Drees' family and recently moved from Colorado to Peshtigo to be near them.

She's also near the cemetery where Drees rests next to his grandfather.

"He would have been the most amazing father in the world," Baker said. "My heart hurts every day when I think about little Steven not getting a chance to ever know his dad."

Periodical and Internet Sources Bibliography

The following articles have been selected to supplement the diverse views presented in this chapter.

Michelle Ainsworth	"Derryn Hinch Slams Australia's Organ Donation Rates," *Herald Sun*, January 17, 2012.
BBC News	"Presumed Consent Plan: Wales Supplies More Organ Donors," October 4, 2011. www.bbc.co.uk.
Belfast Telegraph	"Organ Donation Varies Across UK," October 3, 2011.
Catherine Bolsover	"Three Die a Day in Germany Waiting for an Organ Transplant," Deutsche Welle, June 6, 2011. www.dw.de.
CBC News	"Organ Donation: The Gift of Life," June 25, 2009. www.cbc.ca.
Leigh Dayton	"Organ Donor Rate Lags Despite $150m Funding," *Australian*, December 15, 2011.
Edmonton Journal	"Canada's Organ-Donation Rate Among World's Worst," April 7, 2008.
Branwen Jeffreys	"How the Spanish Donor System Works," BBC News, January 13, 2008. www.bbc.co.uk.
Jane Kirby	"Organ Donations Will Not Hit Target," *Independent*, January 24, 2012.
Nick Lavars	"Alarming Chilean Organ Donor Rate Prompts Government Proposal," *Santiago Times*, January 17, 2012.
Michelle McDonagh	"Tackling the Decline in Organ Donor Rates," *Irish Times*, March 3, 2011.

GLOBAL VIEWPOINTS

CHAPTER 2

Barriers to Organ Donation

American Organ Donations Hindered by Religious and Cultural Myths

Allison Pond

Allison Pond is a reporter for the Deseret News. *In the following viewpoint, she maintains that many Americans do not sign up as organ donors because of cultural and religious myths about organ donation. These beliefs are inaccurate, she says, because no major religion prohibits organ donation. Pond reports that organizations are working to improve education and outreach, especially in minority communities, to inform potential donors about the process and religious teachings on organ donation.*

As you read, consider the following questions:

1. According to Pond, how many people are on the organ donation waiting list in the United States?
2. How many Americans does Pond say die each day waiting for an organ transplant?
3. What organization manages the US organ transplant system under contract with the federal government?

A ngela Siatta, an organ donation coordinator, remembers a Buddhist mother who wrestled with the decision to donate her son's organs when he died.

Allison Pond, "Myths About Religion and Organ Donation Cause Hesitation," *Deseret News*, August 5, 2011. Copyright © 2011 by Deseret News. All rights reserved. Reproduced by permission.

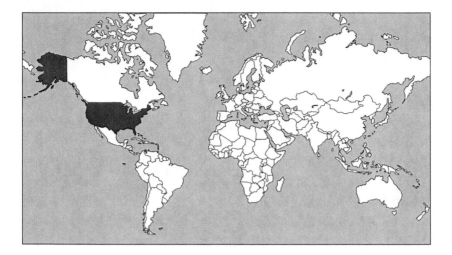

"She said, 'I think it's a great thing, but I'm not sure if it's the right thing for my religion,'" recalled Siatta, a registered nurse who works for Intermountain Donor Services [IDS]. "(Buddhists) believe that the spirit is still with the body until the heart stops. And then the spirit is gone. He was brain dead, and that's a legal definition of death, but because his heart was still beating, she wasn't sure whether his spirit was still there. And so she wanted her Buddhist priest to come and meet with her."

The number of Americans signing up to be organ donors is rising overall, but many are still hesitant—some because of misconceptions about what their religion teaches on the subject.

The priest arrived at the hospital, and after several hours of private conversation in which the religious leader assured the family the young man's spirit was gone and the decision was a personal choice, the mother decided to donate his organs.

"She really wanted to make sure it was the right thing," Siatta said, "and she did feel like it was the right thing after she was able to (speak) with her priest.... It turned out to be a very positive experience for her."

Organ Donations in the United States

The number of Americans signing up to be organ donors is rising overall, but many are still hesitant—some because of misconceptions about what their religion teaches on the subject. Meanwhile, the gap between the number of people waiting for a transplant and the number of organs available is widening.

During the time it takes to read this [viewpoint], another name will be added to the waiting list—something that happens every 11 minutes, according to the U.S. Department of Health and Human Services.

There are currently more than 111,000 people on the list. And while an average of 75 people receive a transplant each day, another 20 people die each day waiting for transplants due to a shortage of donations.

As many as 20 percent of those who decline to be organ donors in Utah and Idaho mention religion, estimates Alex McDonald, director of public education for Intermountain Donor Services, a nonprofit organization that maintains the donor registry for the region.

Religious Beliefs Regarding Organ Donations

And yet, no major religion prohibits organ donation. Some faiths leave the decision up to the individual. Others actively encourage organ and tissue donation as an act of love and charity. Pope Benedict XVI has been outspoken in favor of donation and carried a donor card himself until he assumed the papal throne, according to the Vatican.

Even Jehovah's Witnesses, who believe the Bible prohibits blood transfusions, still allow for organ or tissue donation if all blood is removed before the operation.

Religious Myths Persist

Yet, myths persist about the positions of religious groups on organ and tissue donation. For example, McDonald said, "A lot of people are concerned about the resurrection and feel that they have to have all of their parts to be resurrected." Among non-Christians, like the Buddhist mother, concerns may be different. McDonald said IDS's policy is to encourage people to check with their religious leaders. "Don't take it from us. Please explore and find out," he said.

He also said religious reservations are often not grounded in any specific teachings, but rather represent a more general hesitation.

"A lot of times, when people are uncomfortable with donation but they aren't quite sure why, that's kind of a fallback position because nobody wants to get in an argument about other people's religions, so that's a good way to kind of get out of that discussion," he said.

Donor networks in Texas and Arizona have found that Latinos are considerably less likely to register as organ donors and that their hesitance often has to do with religion. The same has been documented among African-Americans, Polynesians and other ethnic groups.

Joel Newman, assistant director of communications for the national organization United Network for Organ Sharing [UNOS], has had similar experiences discussing organ donation with people.

"I think people have individual spiritual beliefs that are perhaps a little bit different from what the official position of, say, the Catholic Church is. (Some) Catholics may feel that the body needs to stay intact and . . . whole in order to get to heaven," he said.

Other Issues

Newman also suggested that religious issues crop up more often when people haven't discussed organ donation with loved ones ahead of time.

"The greater issue is just that people haven't really thought about it . . . and then something happens and they're placed in that position where, with really no information, they now have to make this very important decision," he said. "I think it's more the fact that the discussion doesn't take place, more than it's, 'Yes, we talked about it, and yes, we think it's against our religion, and no, we're not interested.'"

Culture may also play a role. Donor networks in Texas and Arizona have found that Latinos are considerably less likely to register as organ donors and that their hesitance often has to do with religion. The same has been documented among African-Americans, Polynesians and other ethnic groups. And because matches for organ donation are more common within similar ethnicities, this leaves many minority patients without transplants. In Utah and Idaho, however, consent rates are as high among Hispanics as among the white population, according to McDonald, and he credits IDS's outreach to the Latino community.

"With the Hispanic population, it's really a matter of trust. Do they trust the organization, and do they trust we're telling the truth?" he said. "We have a Spanish-speaking person on our staff, Rocio Mejia, who does education in the Hispanic community and also works with families at the hospital who are Spanish-speaking. She speaks the language, and she is from Mexico, so she understands the culture, so it's not part of the English-speaking white community asking them for their loved ones' organs."

Outreach Efforts

Siatta, the IDS organ donation coordinator, also explained how the donation process is sensitive to cultural and religious

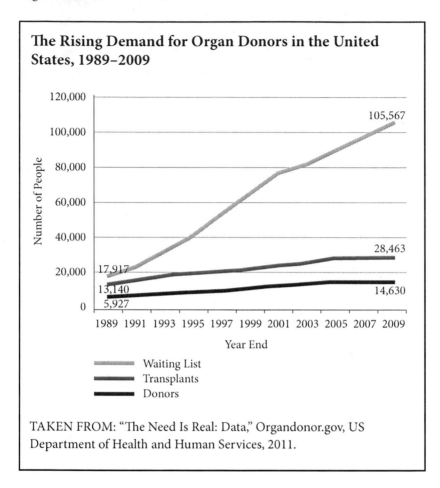

The Rising Demand for Organ Donors in the United States, 1989–2009

120,000

105,567

100,000

80,000

Number of People

60,000

40,000

28,463

20,000
17,917

13,140
5,927

14,630

0

1989 1991 1993 1995 1997 1999 2001 2003 2005 2007 2009

Year End

Waiting List
Transplants
Donors

TAKEN FROM: "The Need Is Real: Data," Organdonor.gov, US Department of Health and Human Services, 2011.

beliefs. "I have had many donor families that are Catholic, especially Hispanic Catholic families who want their loved one to hold the rosary the whole time, even when we go to the operating room," she said. "Those are important things for them, and we'll honor those wishes."

In addition to reaching out to minorities, organ donation groups also engage directly with religious groups.

UNOS, which manages the nation's organ transplant system under contract with the federal government, produces a clergy manual that local organizations like IDS can purchase and share with faith leaders, Newman said.

It also promotes "Donor Sabbath," an event observed two weekends before Thanksgiving in congregations around the country. Local houses of worship bring in guest speakers, preach sermons, publish messages in their bulletins and otherwise encourage parishioners to talk about donation and sign up to be donors.

"It's a very targeted way to try to get that discussion into the faith community," Newman said.

Faith Leaders on Organ Donation

During National Donate Life Month in April, IDS hosted an interfaith panel of religious leaders, including a Baptist minister, an LDS bishop [from the Church of Jesus Christ of Latter-Day Saints], a Catholic priest, a Jewish rabbi and an Episcopal priest. All spoke positively about donation, McDonald said.

For example, Jewish rabbi Ilana Schwartzman said that in the Jewish religion, anything you can do to save a life overrides other religious obligations, McDonald recalled. "I can't remember how many (commandments) they're supposed to follow every day, but if you can save a life, all of that goes out the window because that's the most important thing you can do," he said.

For some others, faith plays yet another role in organ donation.

A Spiritual Blessing

Lucile Jensen's son Conrad passed away 13 years ago. She describes the experience of organ donation as a spiritual blessing during a time of intense pain.

"It's just an impossible time to make any kind of decision. It's a tragedy when things like that happen and usually without a lot of time for you to think about it," she said. "I can't even describe the anxiety and the fear and the dread and the loss and everything—it's just very stressful. Your body and your mind can't think right."

When Jensen and her husband realized the seriousness of Conrad's condition, they walked to her husband's office to offer a prayer together before returning to the hospital to make the excruciating decision.

"I didn't think at the time, 'Is my religion for or against it?' because I felt more than knew that it wasn't against it," she said. Jensen is LDS.

Today, Jensen maintains a relationship with three recipients of Conrad's organs, including Jill Hyde, who received his heart. Seeing Hyde marry and adopt a child has validated the decision to donate, Jensen said.

"My family had incredible experiences," she said. "We would say that (donation) gives you . . . a co-experience with joy as you go through your loss."

VIEWPOINT *2*

Israel's Religious Misconceptions a Barrier to Organ Donation

Calev Ben-David

Calev Ben-David is a journalist. In the following viewpoint, he contends that some health officials in Israel believe that a new law will go a long way in clarifying the confusion on the definition of death. In turn, the law will hopefully spur a rise in the number of organ donations in the country. In recent years, there has been a deadlock between the rabbinate and the medical establishment over the nature of brain death that has exacerbated misunderstandings about death and organ donation. Ben-David reports that there is a need for more education on Jewish edicts on organ donation and what constitutes brain death in human beings.

As you read, consider the following questions:

1. According to Israel's National Transplant Society, what percentage of Israelis with family members suitable to be organ donors refuse to give permission?
2. According to the director of the Halachic Organ Donor Society, how many Israelis a year are left waiting for the organ transplants they need?

Calev Ben-David, "Analyze This: Vital Organs," *Jerusalem Post*, March 25, 2008. Copyright © 2008 by the Jerusalem Post. All rights reserved. Reproduced by permission.

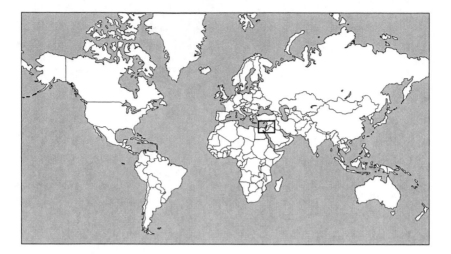

3. How many Israelis die every year from not receiving the organ transplant they need?

Robby Berman, director of the Halachic Organ Donor Society, a nonprofit organization that seeks to encourage organ donation from Jews here and abroad to the general population, is glad that the Knesset [Israeli legislative body] has now passed landmark legislature dealing with this issue. But he is skeptical that the new law will do what its backers claim—spur families of brain-dead loved ones to allow their organs to be donated.

The New Law in Israel

To understand why requires some background about what exactly the new law does, and doesn't, address. What it does do is break a long-standing deadlock between the rabbinate [the religious governing body] and the medical establishment over the exact role of rabbis and doctors in deciding whether a patient is brain dead (that is, the cortex and brain stem no longer function and the brain cells begin to liquefy, with the most immediate result being failure of the lungs).

What the law doesn't do is alter in any way existing medical or religious standards in defining death. According to the

National Transplant Society, a little more than 50 percent of Israelis with family members suitable to be organ donors refuse to give permission for a donation to be carried out.

There are two main reasons for this, says Berman. First, many people do not understand the nature of brain death, and second, they (including much of the secular public) believe that the procedure is absolutely forbidden by Jewish religious law.

What the [Israeli] law doesn't do is alter in any way existing medical or religious standards in defining death.

"People in general don't give permission for organs to be donated from themselves or their loved ones, because they confuse brain death with a coma, and hope for a miracle that the person will wake up," he says. "But brain death is irreversible, and even if somebody is put on a ventilator, there will still be complete systemic failure, including of the heart, in typically no more than a few days."

Unfortunately, lay people, and even many journalists, confuse the issue by referring to ventilators as "life-support" machines. All they do is pump air into the lungs; you can take a corpse and hook it up to a ventilator and pump air through its lungs, but that doesn't mean it's not dead. "So when families hear that their loved ones are hooked up to a 'life-support' system, they are under the mistaken impression they are alive." he says.

Jewish Beliefs Regarding Organ Donations

As for the religious issue, Berman notes that "many leading Orthodox rabbis, including the rabbinate, have long approved organ donations from brain-dead patients, while there are also haredi authorities who still do not. Most religious families

97

who are asked for organ donations consult their rabbis before giving their decision, and I don't foresee this changing as a result of this new legislation."

"What's really needed," he continues, "is a broader educational effort to make the public more aware of the need for organ donors, and of the actual medical and halachic issues involved."

Unfortunately, one part of the bill that was dropped prior to its passing, at the demand of Finance Minister Ronnie Bar-On (Kadima [a political party]), was a provision providing NIS [New Shekel, the currency of Israel] 5 million to fund a public relations campaign informing about and encouraging organ donation. The bill's principle sponsor, Kadima MK [member of the Knesset] Othniel Schneller, believes that the media coverage given its passing will in part help in this regard.

"This is certainly a positive thing and I applaud the effort," responds Berman, who sat in on the subcommittee discussions crafting the bill. "But there are about 1,000 Israelis a year who are left waiting for the organ transplants they need, and about 100 of them die as a result of not getting them. I doubt this legislation by itself will significantly change that."

And what about organ donations from healthy donors? "I get calls every week from Israelis in financial distress, asking about the possibility of donating their kidneys for financial remuneration," says Berman; "But of course I tell them this is against the law."

Organ Trafficking

A secondary law passed in conjunction with the legislation on brain-death organ donations stiffens the penalties for those who look to broker such transactions, including arranging for organ donations abroad. Yet the issue is not so simple; the law does in fact allow for certain financial incentives: compensating organ donors with NIS 18,000; covering any medical costs during and after the donation procedure; permitting them to gain the status of "chronic patient" from the national health funds; and—somewhat absurdly—exempting them from paying the entrance fee to national parks and nature reserves.

This was already too much financial inducement for some opponents of the bill, most notably Labor MK Shelly Yacimovich, who claims it will unfairly promote a trade in human organs from among the working and lower classes. What she doesn't take into account is that wealthier Israelis already can and do take advantage of laxer organ donation laws abroad—for example, payment for kidney donations is legal in the Philippines—to obtain lifesaving transplants elsewhere. According to reliable sources, this group includes the relatives of two current cabinet members—one who recently received a kidney transplant abroad, and another who is in the process of doing so. But those less well-off Israelis who Yacimovich is rightly concerned about don't have that option; their only hope is to increase the organ donor pool here in Israel.

Whether this new legislation will actually succeed in doing so should become clearer over the coming year. If it doesn't, the Knesset and the rabbis will have to look again at this contentious issue, and make some difficult decisions for the sake of the dozens of Israelis who face certain death each year if they cannot obtain the necessary organ transplants.

Japanese Doctors Are Reluctant to Harvest Organs

Natsuko Fukue

Natsuko Fukue is a journalist. In the following viewpoint, she contends that many doctors in Japan are reluctant to harvest organs or lack the knowledge and experience to fully inform patients about organ donation. Although there are donor coordinators in Japan, there is no standard procedure when it comes to talking about organ donation, and coordinators are often unappreciated. The author reports that many officials believe that there needs to be a cultural shift—one that promotes organ transplants and appreciates the people involved in the process—in medical circles when it comes to teaching doctors about organ donations.

As you read, consider the following questions:

1. According to Japanese neurosurgeon Shunichi Yoshikai, what is the main reason that many Japanese doctors are reluctant to harvest organs?

2. How many organ donors were there in Japan in 2008, according to the author?

3. According to the viewpoint, how many organ donations were there in the United States in 2008 from deceased donors?

Natsuko Fukue, "Acceptance of Donating Will Still Take Time," *The Japan Times*, July 14, 2009. Copyright © 2009 by the Japan Times. All rights reserved. Reproduced by permission.

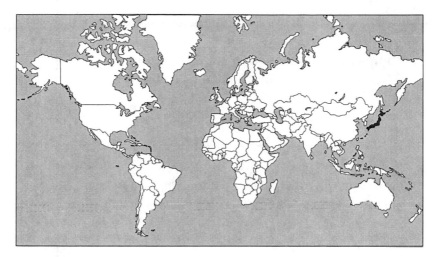

The passage of revised organ transplant legislation Monday [July 13, 2009] may be a big step forward in saving sick children in need of organs, but experts say it will still take time for the ranks of domestic donors to increase.

A Shocking Reluctance

One big reason is that doctors are either reluctant to harvest organs or lack the knowledge on how to tell families of donor candidates about the options, said Shunichi Yoshikai, a neurosurgeon at Shin-Kokura Hospital in Fukuoka Prefecture.

"Many doctors in Japan are reluctant to even learn about organ donations," Yoshikai said. "One of the young doctors even said he thought organs can be donated only when a patient is brain dead."

The New Organ Transplant Law

The organ transplant law until now allowed patients, including children, whose hearts have failed, and people aged 15 and over pronounced brain dead, to be a donor.

Yoshikai pointed out that lack of education is the main reason many Japanese doctors are reluctant to harvest organs.

There are not many lectures in medical colleges on organ donation or transplants, and doctors do not know how to communicate with relatives of candidate donors, he said.

"Nobody told me how to talk with the patient's family about organ donations," said Yoshikai, who has harvested organs from patients whose hearts had stopped.

Although there are donor coordinators in Japan, they have differing approaches. Some explain everything to a patient's family, while others want doctors present when they talk about donating organs. Still others let doctors provide the organ donation option.

When a patient he judges cannot be revived and is a registered donor, he tries to appeal to relatives to get their consent to harvest the person's organs, telling them about the numerous people awaiting organs in Japan.

Donor Coordinators in Japan

Although there are donor coordinators in Japan, they have differing approaches. Some explain everything to a patient's family, while others want doctors present when they talk about donating organs. Still others let doctors provide the organ donation option.

Yoshikai said donor coordinators quit after a few years because they are not paid for the hard work they perform.

"In Spain, there are many organ donors partly because the government invests in donor coordinators," he said.

The Media Creates Difficult Conditions

Another reason donors are few is the media tend to go after doctors when misfortune befalls either organ donors or recipients, Yoshikai said.

"When we see doctors apologizing on TV, we feel like we might be next because we're always engaged in a risky job."

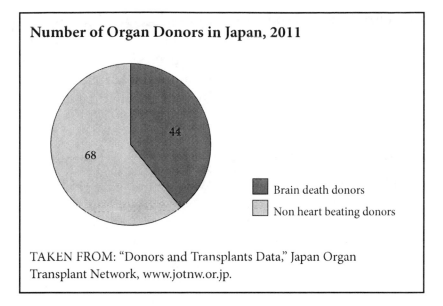

Number of Organ Donors in Japan, 2011

44

68

Brain death donors

Non heart beating donors

TAKEN FROM: "Donors and Transplants Data," Japan Organ Transplant Network, www.jotnw.or.jp.

Due to such conditions, donors have not increased in Japan, reaching only 109 in 2008. Of the patients waiting for an organ, 94 percent are in need of kidneys that can be donated from people whose hearts stopped, as well as from brain-dead patients.

In the U.S., where brain death is recognized as death, there were 7,985 cases of organ donations from the deceased last year [2008].

"The U.S. government has been promoting organ transplants," said Dr. Atsushi Sugitani, who has performed transplants in Pittsburgh.

The U.S. Organ Donation Difference

Sugitani, who now teaches at Fujita Health University in Aichi Prefecture, said medical students in the U.S. learn about brain death, organ donations and transplants at universities, and emergency doctors, brain surgeons and paramedics, including nurses, are trained about organ donations through programs offered by the United Network for Organ Sharing.

Unlike Japan, donor coordinators in the U.S. provide detailed explanations to a patient's family. When the patient does not have a donor card, doctors give options on whether to stop medical treatment, continue until the heart stops even if the patient is brain dead, or agree to donate organs, Sugitani said.

Addressing Misconceptions

Because doctors in the U.S. suggest these three options when a patient is brain dead, there is no misunderstanding. But in Japan, families of patients are still skeptical that doctors may end treatment for the sake of an organ donation even though there may be a way to save the patient.

"It is sad that there is such a misunderstanding in Japan."

Now that the law has changed, expectations are rising that patients waiting for organs will not have to travel overseas for transplants.

However, the number of transplants will not increase in a flash, Yoshikai said.

Obstacles Remain for the Field of Face Transplants

Paul Voosen

Paul Voosen is a journalist. In the following viewpoint, he examines the growing field of facial transplants, a procedure that many surgeons do not try because of the complicated logistical and ethical issues involved. In particular, doctors and ethicists question if the surgery is worth the medical risk. Another obstacle is finding donors. Voosen maintains that most families find facial donation to be a sensitive issue, and the process requires rigorous psychological screening and support for donor families and patients.

As you read, consider the following questions:

1. According to Voosen, in what country did the first face transplant happen?
2. What did England's Royal College of Surgeons recently say about face transplants in a report?
3. How many kidney transplants take place in·Boston every year, according to the author?

S werving ethical pitfalls, Czech doctor to conduct controversial face surgery.

Isabelle Dinoire is thrilled with her new face.

Paul Voosen, "For Transplants, 'God in Details,'" *The Prague Post*, February 20, 2008. Copyright © 2008 by The Prague Post. All rights reserved. Reproduced by permission.

It has been more than two years since Dinoire became the recipient of the world's first partial face transplant in France, after her original mouth and nose were gnawed off by a pet dog concerned by her overdose on sleeping pills. She can now feel the graze of a filament across her cheek and her drooling is under control.

Dinoire's replaced face is well on its way to being a success story, but it did not come without sacrifice or controversy. Twice her body came close to rejecting the foreign skin, which could have led to the face sloughing off. To prevent such rejection, she must take debilitating drugs for the rest of her life.

Since Dinoire's surgery, only two similar transplants have taken place, one in China and the other also in France. Many surgeons are deterred by the logistical and ethical layers enfolding the operation, leaving the field open to a select group of trailblazing doctors who are looking to push the limits of medicine.

One of those surgeons is Bohdan Pomahac, a Czech national working at Brigham and Women's Hospital in Boston, Massachusetts. Pomahac, who directs the hospital's burn unit, is setting up a surgical unit to conduct face transplants, and he could soon become the first to lead the surgery in the United States.

"The bottom line is that the risk [of face transplants] isn't as significant as surgeons thought," Pomahac says.

More than any kind of surgery, facial reconstruction fascinates Pomahac, a point that became clear in a series of phone interviews.

"God is in the details" in face work, he says. "You can really change someone's life."

Saving Face

The face is the crux of human interaction, its variations and symmetries tied into our notions of self, other and beauty.

Should our face be sheered from the latticework of muscle and sinew on which it balances, souls could be set adrift. But, thanks to modern medicine, you could live. Losing face does not mean losing life.

Face transplants, unlike lifesaving kidney or heart transplants, are termed "non-life-threatening" by doctors—they're essentially optional. That is the challenge confronting Pomahac.

The face is the crux of human interaction, its variations and symmetries tied into our notions of self, other and beauty.

While the two types of surgeries differ in perceived need, they're identical in treatment: Both require patients to take cocktails of immunosuppressant drugs for the rest of their lives. Immunosuppressants, as you may expect, reduce the effectiveness of the immune system.

The drugs are a necessary evil. Without them, white blood cells would attack transplanted organs in the body's misguided attempt to defend itself. Sacrificing these defenses, though, means that recipients of organ transplants face increased risks of infection and cancer, potentially shortening their lives by decades, Pomahac says.

The controversy surrounding the first three recipients of face transplants is that, except for their disfigurements, they had healthy immune systems. Now Dinoire, "although she looks great, [will] probably be in the hospital once or twice a year," Pomahac says. People don't quite get "how significant the side effects are," he adds.

With these side effects in mind, many have questioned the ethics of conducting face transplants. Does exposing healthy patients to immunosuppressants violate the bedrock medical principle of primum non nocere—first, do no harm?

"What is the whole world going to say when you start changing people's faces?" says John Barker, a surgeon at the University of Louisville who has conducted similarly optional hand transplants. "What risks would people accept to get one of these non-lifesaving procedures?"

To help answer these questions, Barker led a team that conducted a survey of 400 people wrestling with these questions from various approaches: transplant surgeons, plastic surgeons, the facially disfigured, hand amputees.

"[We asked] basic questions like, how much risk would you accept to get a face transplant?" Barker says. The responses were revelatory. "All of them would risk the most to get a face transplant. They would risk more to get a face than a kidney."

People want to look human. And skin grafts and other forms of plastic surgery used for facial reconstruction just can't produce the same results as transplants, Pomahac says.

In the run-up to Dinoire's surgery, the medical community split on the face transplant question. England's Royal College of Surgeons published a report saying it was "unwise" to proceed with such transplants pending more research. The French went ahead anyway. Last December, they published an update on Dinoire in the *New England Journal of Medicine*, which Pomahac found heartening.

"I don't think there is any way you could achieve this result with conventional means," he says. "Isabelle has the ability to carry on a normal life and you can't say that would be the case for patients with conventionally reconstructed faces."

As he prepares his team to conduct a surgery, Pomahac has worked to address every possible contingency. But there are questions lingering about the operation, he admits: "Some answers you just won't get unless you do it."

An Elegant Solution

The transplant system designed by Pomahac will allow more of these surgeries to take place, while artfully sidestepping many ethical qualms. Most notably, Pomahac will only target patients who are already on immunosuppressants—an elegant solution, Barker says.

"It's a unique situation to have someone who already has immunosuppressants," he says. "There isn't the argument of risk versus benefit."

Boston alone has about 500 kidney transplant patients a year. Pomahac knows that over the past three years several of these patients developed face cancer as a side effect of their immunosuppressant drugs, suffering serious disfigurement. These twice-bitten cancer victims constitute Pomahac's ideal patient.

Unfortunately, Pomahac's criteria make this Platonic patient difficult to find. Since receiving the go-ahead from Brigham and Women's to conduct the surgery late last summer, Pomahac has not found a single patient, he says, partially because such surgeries were not yet ready to move forward.

According to Barker, Pomahac will have difficulty locating patients.

"The key thing there is, where do you find these patients? It's going to be a needle in a haystack," he says. "[But] if they've got them, that's a great opportunity. . . . The more of these cases that are done, the better it is for everyone."

Once he has a list of patients, Pomahac has the rest of his plans prepared. When the call comes from an organ bank with a donor, several teams will go into action. One will "harvest" the face from the donor, who, creepily enough, must still have a heartbeat. Soft tissues are sensitive to loss of blood flow and will die in four hours without blood, Pomahac says.

After being cut from the donor, the face would then be whisked to the waiting patient, where Pomahac would connect, one after another, the face's arteries, veins and muscles to the patient. (The surgery, for all its aura, is not groundbreaking. The technical skills for it have existed for 20 years, Barker says.) At the same time, a second team will graft a piece of the donor's skin to the patient's chest, which will be used for future biopsies. The patient could likely go home after a week, Pomahac says.

When describing the process, Pomahac sounds like the stereotype of detached, surgical precision. He wanted to be a surgeon since entering medical school in Moravia, and he knew that finding emotional disconnection comes with the work. It's necessary. If he saw one of his patients on the street, Pomahac says, he might also say, "My god, that's horrifying. . . . Sometimes it is heartbreaking."

Pomahac's surgeries, like most bleeding-edge operations, won't come without risk. The looming question, says Arthur Caplan, a bioethicist at the University of Pennsylvania, is "what will you do if the experiment fails?" If the face is literally rejected, "would you let someone die under those circumstances?"

Donor Watch

Perhaps the largest challenge facing Pomahac, more so than finding patients, is finding donors. To most people, organs like the kidney and heart are abstractions, the stuff of high school anatomy courses and jars of formaldehyde. The face is different. The face is personal.

Typically, each year there are "at least one or two families who say take anything [from the organ donor] that may possibly help," Pomahac says. He is currently ironing out the regulations overseeing such donations with the New England Organ Bank that he expects the bank board to approve this month.

Pomahac stresses that the families of recently deceased organ donors—the United States has an opt-in system, typically identified on driver's licenses—will not find the face of their loved one surreptitiously harvested for a transplant. Rather, potential donors would have to specifically sign up for the program.

The restricted nature of donors is a vital point and must be widely disseminated, says Caplan.

"You can kill people if you're not careful how you do this," he says.

Fearful of the unknown or reluctant to sacrifice that last visual connection, "you might get people tearing up their organ donor cards," which would prevent lifesaving organs like the kidney from being used.

Perceptions about face transplants could change over time. Pomahac works with the legendary surgeon Joe Murray, who won the Nobel Prize for conducting the first kidney transplant. Murray told Pomahac that he sees many parallels between the two projects. There was public wariness about kidney transplants, but now the procedure is commonplace. If you can give the heart and the liver, why not the face?

To most people, organs like the kidney and heart are abstractions, the stuff of high school anatomy courses and jars of formaldehyde. The face is different. The face is personal.

It changes when talking about full face transplants, which doctors in London and Cincinnati are pursuing. Surgeons know that, with partial transplants, there is little chance the patient will resemble the donor. But, with a full transplant, if the two had similar bone structures, the donor could appear as a walking, talking death mask.

Even for full transplants where this is not the case, the psychological impact would be enormous.

"Seeing a loved one coming back home with a different face would provoke reactions not only from the patient but also the social circle and family," Pomahac says.

Any transplant program would require rigorous psychological screening and social support for donor families and patients, Caplan says. Brigham and Women's will provide such supports, Pomahac says, and, since the program will work with existing patients, the hospital will already know much about their composure.

Both Pomahac and Barker look ahead to a time when the side effects of immunosuppressants are minimal. The drugs have already improved over the decades, and Barker thinks their impact on healthy patients has been exaggerated by dominant medical studies.

Pomahac is more skeptical of this view but remains adamant that transplants represent the future of facial reconstruction. It is the way forward, he says, because the alternatives, like tissue engineering—growing a nose or ear in a dish—are far from reality.

It may bring a yuck factor, but faces can be transplanted now. The surgery will allow disfigured patients to look in the mirror once again, the muscles of their restored mouth pulling their lips upward in the ghost of a smile.

Saudi Arabia Must Confront Cultural and Religious Taboos

Siraj Wahab

Siraj Wahab is a reporter for the Arab News. *In the following viewpoint, he discusses efforts to raise awareness about the issue of organ donation in Saudi Arabia. Wahab reports that activists are developing clear and ethical guidelines on organ transplantation and are forming a charitable organization to educate the public about the importance of organ donation. The author concludes that religious scholars will play a key role in the effort and will be instrumental in addressing misinformation on Islamic views on organ donation.*

As you read, consider the following questions:

1. According to businessman Abdulaziz AlTurki, when did Saudi scholars first start encouraging organ donation?
2. What is an act of "sadaqa jariya"?
3. What was the decision of Grand Mufti Sheikh Muhammad Sayyid Tantawi?

For a young accident victim or chronically ill hospital patient, cultural taboos against organ donations can be a death sentence. Now a group of highly motivated and con-

Siraj Wahab, "Group Seeks Shift on Organ Donations," *Arab News*, May 1, 2009. Copyright © 2009 by Al Bawaba LTD. All rights reserved. Reproduced by permission.

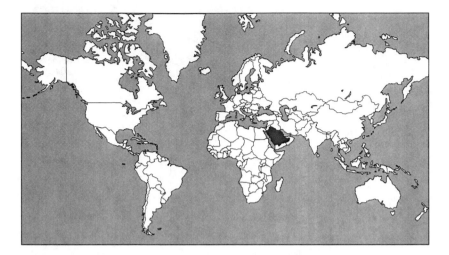

cerned Saudis, led by prominent businessman Abdulaziz Al-Turki, has launched discussions on the creation of a society to raise awareness about the issue in Saudi Arabia.

Donating organs to the sick or injured people is not considered to be an obligation by many in the Arab world and Saudi Arabia in particular. Yet hundreds, if not thousands, of Saudi men, women and children are forced to endure pain and misery in the absence of healthy organs.

Raising Awareness

"This is the need of the hour," AlTurki said at a meeting on the sidelines of the Third International Scientific Conference here yesterday [April 30, 2009]. "There are so many people who are in need of organs to come out of their misery. Some of them are forced to travel abroad, to India and to the Philippines, and to pay an astronomical sum to buy an organ. Not all of them can afford that kind of money. So we thought why not create awareness in our society and to basically encourage people to donate their organs after their death."

He said the concept is still being developed. "We are still deliberating about its composition and its rules and regulations. That is the reason why we invited Dr. Fouad Beydoun, president of the International Association for Organ Donation in the American city of Detroit, and Dr. Faisal Shaheen, director of the Riyadh-based Saudi Center for Organ Transplantation," AlTurki said. "We are venturing in a new area, and we need to learn from the experience of others. We have to have clear-cut guidelines on organ transplantation."

AlTurki said Saudi scholars have encouraged organ donation as far back as 1930. "Sheikh Al-Sadhan urged people to save lives and donate their organs to the needy in 1930s. He would mention these things in his speeches in the Kingdom's mosques during the time. Then we have had rulings from the late Sheikh Bin Baz. He encouraged organ donation, too. In Islam, saving life is more important than anything else."

"A lot of people think organ transplantation is like cutting one hand off and putting it on another."

Bringing Activists Together

Among those who attended yesterday's meeting was former Saudi Aramco executive Bidah Mejdal Al-Gahtani. He is one of the many promoters of the organ-donation campaign. "We've had this in mind for quite some time. We were trying to bring like-minded people together—people who share our concerns and can take the lead in educating the Saudi community about the importance of organ donations. The new society will help organize our efforts," Al-Gahtani said.

He admitted some religious scholars are reluctant to condone organ transplantation. "A small fraction of Saudis are OK with only donating their organs among their close relatives. There is a lot of ignorance about the issue, and there ought to be a sustained campaign to increase awareness in our society," he said. "A lot of people think organ transplantation is like cutting one hand off and putting it on another. They have little or no idea about this critical issue."

Islamic Authorities and Their Support of Organ Donation

Muslim scholars of the most prestigious academies are unanimous in declaring that organ donation is an act of merit and in certain circumstances can be an obligation.

These institutes all call upon Muslims to donate organs for transplantation:

- the Islamic Fiqh Academy of the Organisation of the Islamic Conference (representing all Muslim countries)

- the Grand Ulema Council of Saudi Arabia

- the Iranian religious authority

- the Al-Azhar [University] in Egypt

"Islam and Organ Donation,"
National Health Service Blood and Transplant, 2012.
www.organdonation.nhs.uk. Copyright © 2012
by National Health Service Blood and Transplant.
All rights reserved. Reproduced by permission.

Al-Gahtani said women would be an integral part of the society. "Women are our partners and strong partners, especially when it comes to voluntary work. This is going to be voluntary work. Look at the Saudi Cancer Foundation. There are now more women than men," Al-Gahtani said.

Another member of the yet-to-be-named society is economic researcher Abdullah Al-Alami. "I am here at the invitation of Sheikh AlTurki and Najeeb Al-Zamil, the well-known columnist and member of the Shoura Council," he said. "This is going to be a charitable organization. The religious scholars will have to play a very important role in educating the public about the importance of donating organs. This will save so many lives and will bring so many people out of their current misery," Al-Alami said.

"Sadaqa Jariya"

Talking to *Arab News* on telephone from Cairo, prominent Islamic scholar and well-known medical practitioner Dr. Mohammad Haitham Al-Khayat said organ donation was highly recommended in Islam. "It is a kind of 'sadaqa jariya,' which is essentially an act of charity whose benefits continue after a person passes away," he said, referring to a decision taken by leading Islamic scholars in Kuwait some years ago that endorsed organ donation and organ transplantation.

He said there are differences of opinion regarding organ donation from a person who is clinically dead. "Many of our scholars say one has to be sure that the man or woman is 100 percent dead before his or her organs are taken out for transplantation," he said.

Al-Khayat asked what could be a stronger endorsement than the decision of Al-Azhar's Grand Mufti Sheikh Muhammad Sayyid Tantawi to donate all his organs to the needy. "Yes, he has already made this public. He has donated all his organs to the needy in the event of his death. There should be no confusion after that," Al-Khayat added.

Periodical and Internet Sources Bibliography

The following articles have been selected to supplement the diverse views presented in this chapter.

Julián Aguilar	"Organ Donations Lag in South Texas, and Culture Is a Factor," *New York Times*, March 5, 2011.
Sanjiv Buttoo	"'More Asians Need to Donate Organs,'" BBC News, July 28, 2010. www.bbc.co.uk.
Ruth Gledhill	"Hindu Organ Donor Campaign Begins in London," *Times* (London), July 8, 2011.
Sabria S. Jawhar	"Time for Organ Donation to Be Considered Seriously," *Saudi Gazette*, May 30, 2010.
Jerusalem Post	"Protect Organ Donation," January 2, 2011.
James Key	"More People of Color Needed to Donate Organs," *USA Today*, July 28, 2011.
Andrea Marcela Madambashi	"No Biblical Evidence Against Organ Donation, Says Pastor," *Christian Post*, April 2, 2011.
Jonathan Sacks	"Organ Donor Cards Are Not Incompatible with Jewish Law," *Guardian*, January 13, 2011.
Prerna Sodhi	"Indian Organ Donation Day Marked at AIIMS," *Times of India*, November 29, 2011.
Lucas Sullivan	"Faith Hinders Organ Donations Among Blacks," *Dayton Daily News*, May 3, 2010.
Times of India	"Organ Donation Yet to Catch On in India," June 29, 2011.
Ben Whitelaw	"Transplanting a Culture of Organ Donation," *Guardian*, July 12, 2011.

CHAPTER 3

Strategies to Improve Organ Donations

Canada Should Pay Organ Donors

Erin Anderssen

Erin Anderssen is a feature writer for the Globe & Mail. *In the following viewpoint, she suggests that the idea of compensating organ donors is one that a number of health officials and economists support. Anderssen maintains that a number of countries have put into place financial and other kinds of incentives in order to encourage people to become donors. People should try to look past their own discomfort over the idea and see the benefits, which include eliminating organ trafficking and saving lives. Anderssen concludes that there should be a vigorous debate on the issue in Canada.*

As you read, consider the following questions:

1. According to the author, what country allows people to sell their organs?
2. How much does Anderssen say that Canada will save giving someone on dialysis a transplant?
3. What is one strategy being tried in New York regarding organ transplant teams?

The Internet advertisement reads like a used-car classified: "33 yr old American male. Non smoker or drinker with a clean bill of health. $75,000 U.S. Will travel anywhere. Facility and Physician must meet the highest standard."

Erin Anderssen, "Can Paying for a New Kidney Save Organ Donation?," *Globe & Mail*, June 13, 2011. Reproduced by permission.

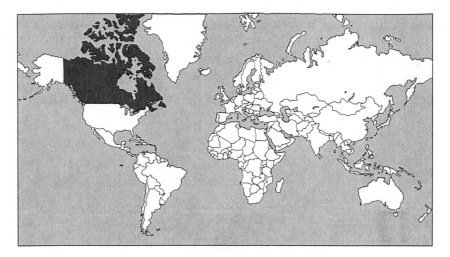

Meet those conditions, and his kidney can be yours.

"This is a rough economy," says the California man who placed the ad, speaking on the condition his name won't be used: What he's doing is illegal. But a good price for a spare organ (plus paid travel and medical expenses) would knock a chunk off the $100,000 he owes on his student loans. A day after placing his latest ad online, he says he has already received 16 e-mails. Eventually, he figures, someone will pay his price for a sturdy, American-bred kidney. Most other sellers on the website say they're from places such as India or Indonesia—organ-trafficking hot spots.

Organ donation is a tragic case of supply not meeting demand, even though transplants have become much safer for recipients and donors.

A Booming Market

The right contact in those countries will find a citizen willing to sell a kidney dirt cheap, by Canadian prices. So if you're rich enough, why wait in line? A quick trip, and you can fly home with your new body part installed (properly, you hope).

121

Good for you, not so good for your donor, who has just received a relative pittance from a broker and now faces questionable follow-up care. And certainly pointless to your fellow Canadians—now numbering about 3,800—who linger on an ever-growing wait list because too few people are willing to give up what they don't need for those who will die without it.

Organ donation is a tragic case of supply not meeting demand, even though transplants have become much safer for recipients and donors. Living Canadians are relatively generous on international rankings, on par with Britain, but our posthumous donations lag far behind leading Spain. Either way, there aren't nearly enough to go around, especially as the population ages. In British Columbia, those who can't afford the international black market can expect to wait an average of nearly six years for a kidney—longer than many patients survive on dialysis.

Incentives?

The best way to bring supply in line, as any economist knows, is to sweeten the deal for the suppliers. So why don't we?

In June [2011], when Canadian Blood Services is due to deliver recommendations on the situation to the provinces, what won't be on the list will be allowing people to profit from the sale of what they clearly own—the parts of their own bodies. It won't even be up for discussion.

However many lives and however much money a market for organs may save, the thought of trading coin for kidney makes too many of us squeamish—that is, until we're watching the slow death of someone we love.

"When something is repugnant to you," Arthur Matas says, "you just keep finding reasons to justify your gut reaction rather than thinking about it."

Dr. Matas is the Canadian-born director of the renal-transplant program at the University of Minnesota and a former president of the American Society of Transplant Surgeons. He has long been a vocal advocate for a broader incentive system for donors that would go beyond covering travel and missed-work expenses, as some provinces do now. (Saskatchewan announced this week that it would provide up to $5,000 to reimburse donors.)

Profiting from organ donations is illegal in most countries, including Canada and the U.S., despite the occasional ad on Craigslist. Iran allows people to sell their organs—receiving cash from both the government and the recipient—and claims to have eliminated its waiting list. And despite prohibitions, an underground market thrives in nations such as China, Egypt and Brazil.

Many countries are already testing the idea of some form of incentive, even if it's not monetary.

A Moral Consideration

Many countries are already testing the idea of some form of incentive, even if it's not monetary. Israel has created a law where people who commit to being donors after they die may jump the line if they or a family member need a new organ themselves. In Britain, consultations are being held to decide where the public stands, for instance, on the idea of covering some funeral expenses for donors. A University of Montreal researcher recently proposed a tax credit for consenting donors that after their death would go to their next of kin.

Would poor people become an organ pool?

The case against allowing people to profit off their organs is usually moral: Critics say it would stop people from giving altruistically, make poor people an organ pool for the wealthy and even encourage the more nefarious among us to hasten the death of unwanted, but organ-rich, relatives. Could someone deep in gambling debts be pressured to give up a kidney?

123

"Okay, Mom. I'm sorry I re-gifted one of the kidneys you gave me," cartoon by Ron Morgan, www.CartoonStock.com. Copyright © Ron Morgan. Reproduction rights obtainable from www.CartoonStock.com.

While donors are rigorously screened, even Dr. Matas concedes that concerns about abuses are legitimate—though safeguards, such as keeping the benefit small, should be part of any debate. "Why do I have to design a perfect system before this concept can be acceptable?" he asks.

The Benefits

Some economists, such as University of Chicago Nobel laureate Gary Becker, argue that something closer to a freely competitive market would stabilize prices and mitigate organ trafficking while recognizing individual freedom. But Dr. Matas envisions a regulated organ market in which governments would determine the compensation for living donors and still control who receives the organs based on need. (At this point he is not including deceased donors, as it's difficult to decide who receives the benefit.)

The cost to taxpayers would be offset by the health care savings: In Canada, statistically, giving someone on dialysis a transplant saves about $50,000 a year.

Under Dr. Matas's system, people would be properly educated about the risks of donation and would receive a financial perk—perhaps in the form of discounted college tuition, or $1,000 each time they go to the doctor for an annual checkup after the operation, as an incentive to take care of their own health as well.

He scoffs at the notion that this would sully the purity of the donor's act of giving. "This concept that donors today are gaining nothing is ridiculous. If your husband is sick and you donate a kidney to him, you benefit from having a healthy husband," he argues. "There are ... other things going on in conventional donation beyond pure altruism. In what other situation do we say that you can do something for free, but you can't do it for an incentive? There is no parallel."

Even the pairing approach to kidney transplants—which allows families to exchange kidneys when they don't match for their own relatives—is a form of transaction. What makes a bonus compensation so different?

Risk and Reward— A Time-Honoured Combination

A large part of the resistance is that compensation such as cash or discounted college tuition is mainly an incentive for lower-income people. "Why is that bad? Poor people do all sorts of things that rich people aren't doing," Dr. Matas says. "Well-informed people are capable of making decisions in their best interest. I won't argue with the fact that billionaires aren't likely do this. So what?"

Altruism doesn't preclude compensation: Society already rewards people such as firefighters and soldiers for taking on dangerous roles that serve the public good. An organ donor is no different, suggests Phil Halloran, a transplant surgeon at the department of medicine at the University of Alberta and the editor in chief of the *American Journal of Transplantation*.

"You are getting paid for what you do," he says. "Surgeons get paid for what they do. Health care works on the basis of people providing good services to other people—and they get paid."

The Risk of Exploitation

As for the risk of exploitation, he argues that people are already receiving unequal care because organs are in shorter supply in certain locations and because the wealthy can seek out other options.

Other experts, such as University of Toronto bioethicist Linda Wright, say Canada should consider some other options first—ones that might be sold more easily to the public, including doing a better job of promoting the idea of organ donation.

Canadian Blood Services hopes to get a national waiting list for organ donations up and running this year—the current one, astonishingly, is still maintained manually by the London Health Sciences Centre in London, Ont., and then faxed out to hospitals.

New Strategies

A key recommendation of the agency's report in June will be to improve frontline resources and personnel in emergency rooms and intensive-care units so that donors can be identified more quickly and families counselled to reach an informed decision—a top priority for Dr. Halloran, and the main factor credited with Spain's high donation rate. (One option that is being tried in New York won't be considered here: having transplant teams in "organ preservation units" trail ambulances responding to 911 calls.)

Some European countries have adopted an opt-out system—in which, with some caveats, people have to alert the government that they will not be donors. However, Canadians are divided on this approach, so it's also not being considered.

"It's really a trust factor," says Peter Nickerson, executive medical director of organ transplantation at Canadian Blood Services. For the system to work, he says, people need to believe that the final choice is theirs.

Prof. Wright, the bioethicist, says people still want organ donation to be "an altruistic act and not for payment." But altruism isn't getting the job done. And Dr. Matas argues that it's wrong that such idealism has kept the idea of compensation for organs from being tested with a government pilot project—or even seriously debated.

Shouldn't we find the status quo equally distressing? "If we don't do something," he says fiercely, "the waiting lists are going to get longer and more of our patients are going to die every day."

The British Hindu Community Is Addressing the Shortage of Organ Donors

Tarun Patel

Tarun Patel is a journalist. In the following viewpoint, he promotes efforts in Britain that aim to address the low rate of organ donations in Hindu communities. Key to such efforts is confronting the cultural or religious myths that stop Hindus from becoming organ donors. Patel contends that by working with leaders from South Asian and Hindu communities, activists and health officials hope to inspire communities to improve organ donation rates and raise awareness about the importance of donation.

As you read, consider the following questions:

1. How many people does Patel say are on the national organ donor register in Britain?
2. According to the author, what percentage of the people on the national organ donor register are from an Asian background?
3. What percentage of the people in Britain waiting for an organ transplant are from a black or Asian background?

Tarun Patel, "Organ Donation and Hindus: Mother-of-Two Begs to Be Given the 'Gift of Life,'" *The Times* (London), July 8, 2011. Copyright © 2011 by News International Syndicate. All rights reserved. Reproduced by permission.

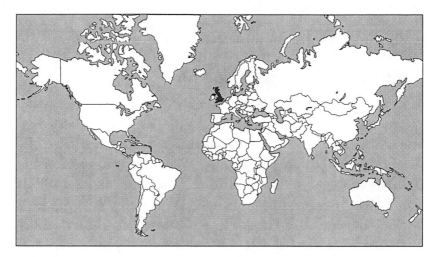

Most people waiting for an organ transplant need a kidney. While kidney failure is not usually life threatening, it causes huge problems and numerous symptoms, and significantly affects the quality of life for the patient and those around them. For people who need another type of organ transplant, such as heart, liver or lung, it is probably their last hope and without a transplant they are likely to die.

Happy Ending

Kirit Modi, 59, former assistant director for education in Luton and Islington, was one of the lucky ones.

Kirit had high blood pressure while in his twenties, which became uncontrollable despite medication, and was found to have resulted from kidney failure. He had two choices, either dialysis which meant a drastic change to his lifestyle and career, or a kidney transplant. His siblings could not help because of their health.

Kirit says: 'I went on the transplant waiting list but people from minority backgrounds have less chance of getting a match. Fortunately, my wife, Meena, offered me one of her kidneys. It really was the gift of life. But I would have done the same for her. We are both well and will be celebrating the tenth year of the transplant later on this year.'

Waiting for Her Happy Ending

Priti Patel ... has not been so lucky. She is currently on the transplant waiting list for a lung. She is a mother of two young daughters and her day-to-day life is severely affected by her ill health. Ethnic background has a big influence on the diseases that people are prone to. For example, people of South Asian origin are more likely to develop diabetes and high blood pressure. These diseases can cause kidney failure and the majority of patients waiting for an organ need a kidney transplant.

As a successful match is more likely to be found from the same ethnic group there is an urgent need for more black and Asian donors. Although 18 million people are registered on the national organ donor register, only 1.3 per cent of these are from an Asian background. In contrast, of the 8,000 people awaiting an organ for transplant, approximately 2,000, or 25 per cent, are from a black or Asian background.

Raising Awareness

This startling statistic was the springboard that brought a few like-minded people together. Kirit Modi, vice chairman of the National Kidney Federation and member of the Lister Kidney Foundation, and Bharti Tailor, secretary general of the Hindu Forum of Britain, linked up with BAPS Charities and the Hindu Healthcare Society to orchestrate a project to tackle the issues preventing Hindus and South Asians from signing up to the organ donation register.

An information leaflet, DVD and the first national conference on organ donation awareness within the Hindu community have been organised. The conference is to take place on 9 July 2011 at the BAPS Shri Swaminarayan Mandir (popularly known as the Neasden Temple).

Hinduism and Organ Donation

According to the Hindu Temple Society of North America, Hindus are not prohibited by religious law from donating their organs. This act is an individual's decision. H.L. Trivedi, in *Transplantation Proceedings*, stated that, "Hindu mythology has stories in which the parts of the human body are used for the benefit of other humans and society. There is nothing in the Hindu religion indicating that parts of humans, dead or alive, cannot be used to alleviate the suffering of other humans."

"Understanding Donation:
Religion and Organ and Tissue Donation,"
The Gift of a Lifetime, originally taken from Organ and Tissue Donation: A Reference Guide for Clergy, *2000.*
www.organtransplants.org.

The project is being supported by a grant from the Department of Health and has been organised in partnership with them. Ms Bharti Tailor describes the statistics as worrying and unacceptable. She said: 'In an age where healthcare provision has improved, miraculous technology is saving people's lives and people are living longer, those that live with a lesser quality of life or perhaps lose their lives simply because of a lack of donors is unfair, undignified and unacceptable.'

Hinduism and Organ Donation

Hinduism is fully supportive of organ donation, and yet people of Hindu and South Asian origin remain reluctant to sign up to the organ donor register. The aim of this conference is to tackle the issues, whether cultural or religious, that may be stopping Hindus and people of South Asian origin from becoming organ donors.

The audience will consist of Hindu patients, leaders of Hindu religious organisations, and leaders of South Asian community organisations. The aim is to inform the leaders of the importance of encouraging their communities to become aware of the need to sign up to the organ donation register, and to have the confidence to tackle potential difficult ethical, cultural, or religious issues that may be raised.

> *Hinduism is fully supportive of organ donation, and yet people of Hindu and South Asian origin remain reluctant to sign up to the organ donor register.*

The conference will request Hindu organisations and individuals to make a pledge of what they will do to tackle the challenges facing our communities.

Providing Solutions

Head of BAPS Healthcare and volunteer of BAPS Charities, Dr Sejal Saglani, explains the campaign will focus on the importance of organ donation, 'The Hindu Forum of Britain and the Hindu Healthcare Society along with BAPS Charities will tackle and champion this important concern within the Hindu community. We must ensure that our efforts translate into tangible benefits and support for those that need organs.' Dr Diviash Thakrar of the Hindu Healthcare Society said: 'The figures are worrying, and we must all work together to resolve the problem. We cannot afford to stand by and leave the matter as it is, hoping that it will go away. It is a very important issue and we fully appreciate the enormity of the task; however, we must attempt to tackle the problem.' We need to ensure Priti will also become one of the lucky ones. Only time will tell.

Wales Is Switching to a Presumed Consent System for Organ Donations

Tracy McVeigh

Tracy McVeigh is the chief reporter for the Observer. *In the following viewpoint, McVeigh examines the switch from an "opt-in" donor card system in Wales to a presumed consent system, which assumes that every person has consented to organ donation after their death unless the person has explicitly indicated otherwise or their relatives object. Health officials predict that this switch will increase the number of organ donations significantly and will save the lives of thousands of people. McVeigh reports that Welsh legislators are taking great pains to respect the wishes of families while making it easier to harvest organs for patients who really need them.*

As you read, consider the following questions:

1. What percentage of the British population is on the national donor register, according to McVeigh?
2. How many people in Wales does the author say die every eleven days waiting for an organ to become available?

Tracy McVeigh, "'Opt-Out' Organ Donation Plan Offers Hope to Transplant Patients in Wales," *The Observer*, May 8, 2010. Copyright © 2010 the Guardian Newspaper. All rights reserved. Reproduced by permission.

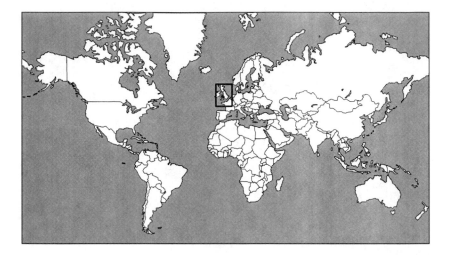

3. According to estimates by the *British Medical Journal*, by
   how much would the number of available organs rise if
   Wales switched to a presumed consent system?

In a television advertisement to be aired in Wales this month
[May 2010], Kerrianne Phillips is filmed in her hospital bed
as if it were on death row.

The tiny side room that she shares with piles of sweet
wrappers, paperbacks and magazines—and her teddy bear pil-
low case "brought from home"—appears to be only a step up
from a cell. "I have spent half my life in hospital," she says.
"This time it's been seven months. Every tiny infection and
I'm back in—it's horrendous."

Born with a liver disease, as a baby she was given weeks to
live, a prognosis repeated throughout her life. Looking younger
than her 22 years, Phillips hates the way in which old ladies
around the hospital mistake her for a pregnant teenager. "It's
not my fault I have this huge stomach. My liver weighs two
stone. It's growing every week, wrapping around my kidneys
and resting on my pelvis. It hurts, and I can't lie flat or it
presses into my diaphragm and I can't breathe."

A drip injects a steady level of morphine into her arm and a feeding tube in her nose keeps her sugar levels regular. She is waiting for a transplant. "It could be another seven months, or a year," she shrugs. "I'm on the priority list, but it's difficult not knowing."

[Lawyers] acting for the Welsh assembly, with cross-party support, are examining its legislative powers to ensure that the country can switch to a "soft opt-out" system—where consent is presumed unless the person has indicated otherwise or their relatives object—by the spring of [2011].

A Policy Change

If ambitious plans to make Wales the first country in the British Isles to change its policy on organ donations come to fruition, Phillips's transplant might come sooner rather than later.

Despite decades of campaigning, only 28% of the British population is on the donor register. Nearly 8,000 people are currently waiting for a transplant and three of them die every week. In Wales one of those people dies every 11 days.

Last week the *British Medical Journal* published a conservative estimate that the number of available organs would rise by 30% if there were a switch to presumed consent instead of the present "opt-in" donor card system. Now lawyers acting for the Welsh assembly, with cross-party support, are examining its legislative powers to ensure that the country can switch to a "soft opt-out" system—where consent is presumed unless the person has indicated otherwise or their relatives object—by the spring of next year [2011]. A consultation has already shown wide support and the plans would be backed up by a specialist transplant unit to be built in Wales.

Opting Out and Consulting with Family

Under a system of "opting out" or "presumed consent," every person living in that country is deemed to have given their consent to organ donation unless they have specifically "opted out" by recording in writing their unwillingness to give organs. . . .

If an individual does not register an objection, it is possible that their silence may indicate a lack of understanding rather than agreement with the policy. It is because of these concerns that in the majority of countries operating an opt-out system, health care professionals still consult the family to establish consent.

"Opt In or Opt Out,"
National Health Service Blood and Transplant, 2008.
www.organdonation.nhs.uk.

Interminable Waiting

In Bronglais [General] Hospital in Aberystwyth, Phillips is constantly moved around the building as staff try to accommodate such a long-term patient. If a liver is found, she would be transferred to Birmingham for the transplant.

"This side room is better than the wards; you can see the sea," says Phillips. "It's all old people [here]. In the past six months I've seen four people under the age of 40, but I like speaking to the old people; it can be interesting. It's nice to hear how times have changed, but a lot of the ones with kidney infections can be doolally. There was one woman who kept seeing green monsters, and then there's the ones who shout all night. I've been woken by people sitting on my bed a few times.

"I used to get bored," she says, "but now I get into my own little bubble—I've got my laptop and games console and I read a lot of books. It's rare for me to go a day without seeing someone. My mum tries to come up after work."

Phillips finds it difficult to imagine what life might be like as a healthy young woman. "People say to me, 'Oh you'll be back to the normal Kerrianne after you get a transplant', but it's scary. I look at all this—skinny arms and legs and this pregnant stomach and these tubes and drugs—and I think this is what's normal; this is Kerrianne."

Presumed Consent

The first minister for Wales, Carwyn Jones, told the *Observer* that he hoped opt-out could be in place before the Welsh assembly elections next spring. "We have decided on soft presumed consent, where relatives can veto organ donation, because we want to make it as easy as possible," he said.

"At the moment, if people are not carrying donor cards then it is presumed they didn't want to be a donor. If we presume everyone does—unless certain conditions are met—we don't want to be in a position where we are taking organs against the wishes of the family. There is no question of that."

Any Welsh person dying outside the country would not come under the scheme unless relatives were available to give consent. Likewise, a hospital would have to consult the family of anyone non-Welsh who died inside the country. Organs would never be taken from someone whose family could not be traced.

The Kidney Wales Foundation, which has produced the new adverts to open public debate, said the details of organ allocation would be sorted out as the system was introduced. Roy Thomas, executive chairman of the foundation, said the Welsh move "threw down the gauntlet to the rest of the UK to follow suit".

However, the process may still take too long to help Kerrianne.

Germany Initiates a Campaign to Raise Awareness of Organ Donation Shortfall

Cinnamon Nippard

Cinnamon Nippard is a journalist. In the following viewpoint, she looks at a new ad campaign in Germany utilizing well-known celebrities to encourage people to become organ donors. The donation rates in the country have been steadily dropping, and health officials blame an ignorance of the importance of organ donation and a lack of infrastructure, especially organ transplant coordinators and other designated staff who identify potential donors early. Nippard maintains that switching to a presumed consent system would also increase the number of organs available for transplantation.

As you read, consider the following questions:

1. What percentage of Germans have become organ donors, according to Nippard?
2. How many Germans does the author say are waiting for organ transplants?
3. According to Nippard, what European country is the world leader in organ transplants?

Cinnamon Nippard, "Drive for More Donors in Germany," *Deutsche Welle*, August 6, 2010. Copyright © 2010 by Al Bawaba LTD. All rights reserved. Reproduced by permission.

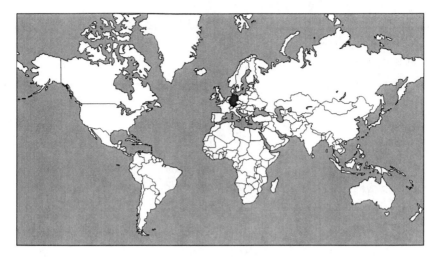

In Germany, donating your organs is voluntary, and while around 60 percent of people say they think it's a good idea, just 14 to 17 percent of them have become organ donors. Advocacy groups are trying to raise awareness about the problem and encourage people to become donors.

There are currently some 12,000 people waiting for organ transplants in Germany and each year between 2 and 3,000 of them will die before they can make it to the top of the list.

According to the British National Health Service, organ transplantation is the most cost-effective treatment for end-stage renal failure. For end-stage failure of organs such as the liver, lung and heart, transplantation is in fact the only available treatment.

Lack of Awareness

There's a poster campaign all over Berlin featuring well-known celebrities to try to raise awareness about organ donation, so it seems surprising that some people haven't heard about it.

Before she had a heart transplant, Ute Opper, 45, would have been among them.

"I did not know anybody who needed an organ. Nobody talked with us. Not in school, and not when I did my driving license," she said.

17 years ago Opper suddenly became seriously ill just four weeks before her wedding; [she was] diagnosed with endocarditis, an inflammation of the heart muscle. After a failed operation on the infected valve led to a heart attack, she was told that her chance of survival required a heart transplant. Opper was lucky and only had to wait a year to receive her new heart.

After this experience, Opper and other patients created a self-help group to support people waiting for organ transplants. She also educates the public to "try to make people who never thought about that, think about it."

"We want to have people imagine you also could be ill and maybe you would need an organ," she said.

Addressing the Problem

Despite the introduction of the German transplant law in 1997, the rates of organ donation in Germany have been steadily dropping. According to Professor Dr Roland Hetzer, director of the German Heart Institute in Berlin, there are two main reasons for this. The first is convincing the public that organ donation is a good idea, while the other problem is a lack of infrastructure.

"Not all hospitals cooperate well enough in reporting brain-dead people who would be potentially an organ donor," said Hetzer, "and this obviously has to do with the increasing economic problems that hospitals are faced with."

Spain is the world leader, not only due to its model of presumed consent, but because it has designated staff that only deal with organ donations. Dr Hetzer believes that Germany would have a higher number of transplants if it too had designated staff.

Eurotransplant Statistics

15,510 patients on the active organ waiting list on January 1, 2012

11,168 registrations on the waiting list in 2011

6,545 organ transplants from deceased donors in 2011

124.7 million inhabitants in the Eurotransplant region (Austria, Belgium, Croatia, Germany, Luxembourg, the Netherlands, and Slovenia)

"About Eurotransplant: Key Figures,"
Eurotransplant, 2012. www.eurotransplant.org.

Controversy

Cardiac surgeon, Dr Reinhard Daniel Pregla, is working hard on public campaigns to increase the number of organ donors in Germany, but at the same time he would like to see the EU [European Union]-wide adoption of stronger models like that of presumed consent used in Spain, Austria and Belgium, or Israel's new law that prioritises organ donors.

Across the European Union there are 60,000 people waiting for organ transplants. According to Dr Pregla every citizen in the EU should have to decide [whether] he or she wants to be an organ donor.

"And if he denies to be an organ donor it should have the consequence that he has less right to receive an organ," he said. "Not that he should not receive an organ, but the priority should be more on those people who are willing to donate organs."

Dr Pregla said that one person can save the lives of five others and that people need to take that into consideration.

"This has to be valued if people decide to do this. It can't be that in general we have the right to take, but not the duty to give. This has to be connected in some way," he said.

Rights of the Individual

Such models have been proposed before, but Dr Hetzer said they are regarded as unconstitutional in Germany, where the right of the individual is clearly outlined in the constitution.

Even though Ute Opper agrees that the Israeli policy and that of presumed consent helps gravely sick people waiting for organs, in her opinion she believes that it's better to educate and inform people and to give them the right to choose.

"It's a gift. A new organ is a gift. And you should say it's my body and if I want to give something away I think I should say that I want to do it," said Opper.

With so many people desperate for organs, some who have sufficient funds turn to the black market.

EU Directive

Things are changing in Europe. The EU Directive on Organ Donation and Transplantation, approved last month [in July 2010], aims to standardize organ procurement and traceability, thereby increasing the availability of organs across the 27 EU member states and reducing organ trafficking.

With so many people desperate for organs, some who have sufficient funds turn to the black market. Freelance journalist, Seema Sanghi, says that perhaps if more people gave their consent to donate their organs, maybe it would stop organ trafficking in places like India where people from the villages move to the cities with the promise of work.

"Then they're knocked out and their organs are taken out without them knowing," Sanghi explained.

While the EU directive, which will be implemented across the member states over the next two years, will have no direct effect on how organ donations are procured in places like India, people like Sanghi hope making [it] easier for Westerners to get a new heart or lung will take pressure off the developing world.

England Is Right to Propose a Presumed Consent Model

Martin O'Neill

Martin O'Neill is an author, professor, and political philosopher. In the following viewpoint, he considers the switch to a presumed consent organ donation system in the United Kingdom to be a win-win policy for Britain. O'Neill argues that the new policy will increase substantially the number of organs available for transplantation without infringing on the rights of families, who can "opt out" of organ donation. O'Neill contends that governments and policy makers should be looking out for more win-win policies like this one, which will end up saving numerous lives every year.

As you read, consider the following questions:

1. How many transplants per million people occur in the United Kingdom every year?
2. According to the author, how many lives could be saved every year if there were enough organs for transplant?
3. What European country does O'Neill say has a "soft" opt-out organ donation system?

Martin O'Neill, "The Ethics of Organ Transplantation," *New Statesman*, January 16, 2008. Copyright © 2008 by the New Statesman. All rights reserved. Reproduced by permission.

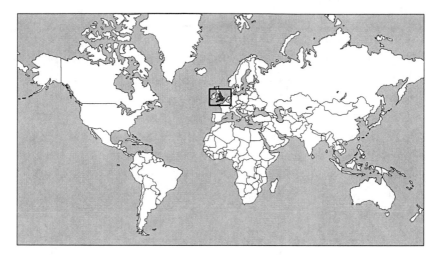

Most political decisions involve trade-offs between different interest groups. Changes in the tax system, for example, typically leave some better off and others worse off. Even when trade-offs between different individuals aren't at stake, political decisions will be a balancing act between different values.

For example, airport security restrictions limit our freedom, in at least the hope of increasing our physical security; those who benefit are the same as those who bear the costs, but everyone has to take a loss (of freedom) in order to create a gain in security.

A Win-Win Situation

What is remarkable about the government's new 'presumed consent' proposals on organ transplantation is that they involve no such trade-offs. No one will be made worse off in any way, although others will benefit, and no important value is sacrificed in pursuit of some other goal. It's a rare case of the sort of 'win-win' solution that governments may occasionally hope to find to difficult political problems. We should support these kinds of 'win-win' policies wherever they crop up, and governments should do more to identify them in other areas.

At the moment, organ transplantation in the UK [United Kingdom] is based on an 'opt-in' system. Organs are harvested for use in transplants only when the dead individual was a carrier of a donor card, or where the individual's family has volunteered his or her organs for use.

This contrasts with the system in countries like Spain, where there is 'presumed consent' for everyone to give their organs for use in transplants. Individuals remain free to opt out of these arrangements if they so wish, and families retain the right to refuse permission for their loved one's organs to be harvested.

It's a rare case of the sort of 'win-win' solution that governments may occasionally hope to find to difficult political problems. We should support these kinds of 'win-win' policies wherever they crop up, and governments should do more to identify them in other areas.

Put simply, in answer to the question of whether a dying person's organs will be available for transplant, the default answer in Spain is 'Yes', whereas the default answer in the UK is 'No'.

The Benefits of Presumed Consent

Unsurprisingly, this difference in the 'default position' has a large influence on the number of transplants that are actually carried out each year in the two countries. In Spain the figure is 33.8 per million of population, whereas in the UK it is just 12.9 per million.

Accordingly, thousands of people in the UK are waiting for organ transplants, and many will die before the end of their wait. If enough organs for transplant could be found, about 1,000 extra lives could be saved every year.

The government's chief medical officer Sir Liam Donaldson backs the move to the Spanish model of 'presumed consent', as does the government's task force on organ dona-

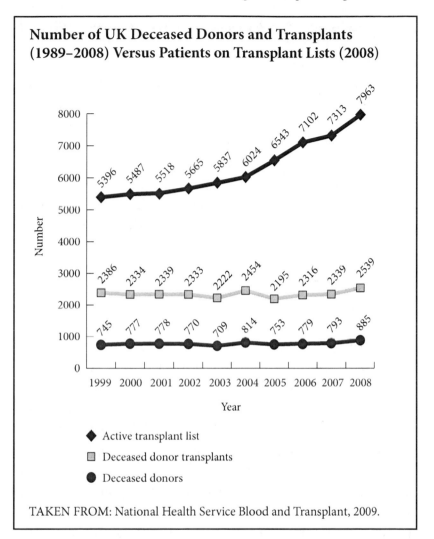

Number of UK Deceased Donors and Transplants (1989–2008) Versus Patients on Transplant Lists (2008)

TAKEN FROM: National Health Service Blood and Transplant, 2009.

tion. It looks like we can expect the Brown government [referring to the government under Prime Minister Gordon Brown] to bring in a thoroughly sensible change of policy following these recommendations, thereby saving hundreds of lives every year.

Donation Infrastructure

As well as the move towards 'presumed consent', the UK will also be adopting something closer to the Spanish model of having highly trained 'organ procurement officers', who will deal with relatives at the fraught but crucial time just before and just after death. (To see such a 'procurement officer' at work, and to see how deep this culture of organ donation now runs in Spanish society, it is instructive to watch Pedro Almodóvar's wonderful film *All About My Mother*, in which the central character, Manuela, works as a procurement officer.)

The move to the Spanish model of 'presumed consent' is a win-win situation because it makes many people better off (i.e., those who will receive organs), whilst leaving no one worse off. Indeed, by relieving some of the pressure on the difficult decision of whether to donate, it arguably makes things somewhat easier for family members. So, everyone benefits. It also involves no trade-offs in terms of values because it increases the life expectancy and quality of life of organ recipients without restricting the freedom of choice of anyone else. Donors and their families still have the entitlement to withhold organs, for whatever reason, and so they face no limitation on their freedom. It is just that 'default position' against which they make their choice has been changed.

The Spanish model with its 'soft' opt-out thereby contrasts with 'hard' opt-out in operation in Austria, where family members are not consulted. Perhaps the Austrian policy is the best option . . . but, by curtailing the freedom of choice of family members, it does not have the 'win-win' structure of the Spanish model.

These sorts of win-win policies can crop up all over the place. For example, some American corporations found that, where they offered their employees a huge range of investment products for their retirement savings, the choice was simply too bewildering, and employees instead chose to save nothing. Too much choice, after all, is useless when we do not have the right kind of information at our fingertips. What such companies have instead done is to sign up their employees for a sensible and prudent investment plan as the default option, whilst still leaving them the full entitlement to 'opt out' of that plan, or to transfer to an alternative.

Libertarian Paternalism

The American legal theorist Cass Sunstein has called these sorts of policies forms of 'libertarian paternalism'—'libertarian' because no one's freedom of choice is affected, but nevertheless a form of 'paternalism' because the well-being of individuals is helped directly by the policy. These sorts of 'libertarian paternalist' policies are the 'one-person' version of the many-person 'win-win' policy involved in the Spanish model of organ donation. Individuals gain in terms of their future well-being, but lose nothing in terms of freedom, because they can still choose to do whatever they were entitled to do before.

The lessons of the 'Spanish model' are twofold. Firstly, one can do a lot in health policy and social policy just by manipulating what the default option might be, without interfering with anyone's freedom of choice. Secondly, although politics is usually about making tough choices, the existence of these kinds of 'win-win' policies means that sometimes doing the right thing in politics can be surprisingly easy.

The United States Should Consider a Mandatory Organ Donation Policy

Scott Carney

Scott Carney is an investigative journalist. In the following viewpoint, he reports that several leading bioethicists and doctors are arguing in favor of a mandatory organ donation policy that would make harvesting organs after death a routine procedure. There are obvious obstacles to such a policy, including beliefs about sanctity of the body, but it might be the only policy that could effectively address the need for organs for transplantation and curb organ trafficking. Carney suggests that if a mandatory organ donation policy is too controversial right now, the United States should consider a presumed consent model, which has had much success in Spain and other countries.

As you read, consider the following questions:

1. According to the author, how many people around the world suffer from kidney failure?
2. According to a 2005 Gallup poll, how many Americans were willing to donate organs after death?
3. How many countries does the author say have a mandatory organ donation policy?

Scott Carney, "The Case for Mandatory Organ Donation," Wired.com, May 8, 2007. Copyright © 2007 Conde Nast Publications. All rights reserved. Originally published in Wired.com. Reprinted by permission.

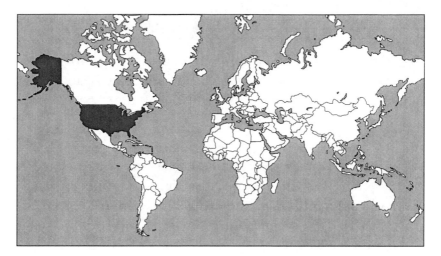

Curbing the illegal trade in human organs just might mean scrapping the way we think about the rights of brain-dead organ donors.

Organ brokers have already proven that they are savvy enough to skirt legal roadblocks, and their businesses will continue as the supply of available donor organs remains small and the profits high.

Increasing the supply of cadaver organs is an obvious solution, but volunteer programs have not produced enough organs to make a difference. Now some leading ethicists and doctors are reexamining the principle of informed consent in government organ donor programs, arguing that harvesting from cadavers should be a routine procedure just like autopsies in murder investigations.

"Routine recovery would be much simpler and cheaper to implement than proposals designed to stimulate consent because there would be no need for donor registries, no need to train requestors, no need for stringent government regulation, no need to consider paying for organs, and no need for permanent public education campaigns," wrote Aaron Spital, a clinical professor at Mount Sinai School of Medicine, and James Stacey Taylor, an assistant professor of philosophy at

151

the College of New Jersey, in a controversial article published this year [2007] by the American Society of Nephrology.

This approach faces obvious and enormous obstacles, challenging as it does widely and deeply held beliefs about the sanctity of the body, even in death. But it could be the only solution that works.

Now some leading ethicists and doctors are reexamining the principle of informed consent in government organ donor programs, arguing that harvesting from cadavers should be a routine procedure just like autopsies in murder investigations.

Roughly half a million people around the world suffer from kidney failure and many are willing to pay any price for a donor organ. They have two options: wait on impossibly long donation lists or pay someone for a live donor transplant.

The United Network for Organ Sharing, which runs the current system of cadaver donation in the United States, maintains lists of brain-dead patients around the country and actively tries to match up prospective donors. At present there are more than 90,000 people waiting for kidneys but only about 14,000 donors enter the system each year.

The shortage of donors isn't based on a shortage of brain-dead people in hospitals, but on the shortage of people whose organs—even after they have opted into a convoluted and difficult organ donation program—never find their way to a viable patient. A 2005 Gallup poll revealed that more than half the population of the United States was willing to donate organs after death, but inefficiencies in the current system mean that even willing donors often end up not donating because families raise objections or there is a question about consent.

Fewer than two out of 10 families opt to donate organs of relatives after death. Hospitals often are unwilling to share organs from donors on their rolls and waste organs while waiting to set up their own in-house transplants. Often, perfectly good transplant organs get lost in a bureaucratic shuffle.

Routine organ donations would dramatically increase the supply of donor organs; with a little effort it would be possible to set up a system to transport donation-worthy organs anywhere in the world.

Once removed from a body, a kidney has a 72-hour window before it needs to be transplanted into a patient. If we use FedEx as our yardstick, with the right transportation infrastructure, that kidney can travel to any point on the globe in less than 24 hours—giving surgeons on either end of the transplant team two days to find a viable donor and perform the necessary surgery. And once regulations for transporting human organs cut through red tape, the cost of transportation would be less than a first-class plane ticket.

The shortage of donors isn't based on a shortage of brain-dead people in hospitals, but on the shortage of people whose organs—even after they have opted into a convoluted and difficult organ donation program—never find their way to a viable patient.

"Bold proposals like those posited by (Spital and Taylor) are necessary to fuel spirited debate and influence public policy. From an ethical view, much of what they have written can be supported and resonates well with some who contemplate such issues," wrote Ron Gimbel, assistant professor in the preventive medicine and biometrics department at the Uniformed Services University of the Health Sciences in Bethesda, Maryland, in an e-mail conversation with Wired News.

Setting up a mandatory system of organ donation would undoubtedly stir protests from around the country. Americans are used to the idea of having a choice over the state of our

**US Transplants Performed Between
January and October, 2011**

Living Donor	4,932
Deceased Donor	18,813
Total	23,745

Based on Organ Procurement and Transplantation
Network data as of 01/06/2012.

TAKEN FROM: Organ Procurement and
Transplantation Network, US Department of
Health and Human Services,
http://optn.transplant.hrsa.gov.

bodies after death and many people would be irked that the
government would be meddling into some of the most sensitive and private moments of a family's life.

In fact, that concept is an illusion. In cases where the
cause of death is ambiguous, the government routinely conducts autopsies where large pieces of the person's viscera are
removed for scientific analysis—often later to be used in a
criminal investigation. In addition, as Spital and Taylor argue,
the government reserves the right to draft young men against
their will into war and risk their lives in combat operations.

Nancy Scheper-Hughes, a medical anthropologist at the
University of California at Berkeley who has made her career
writing about violence caused by poverty, stresses that the
current system of organ donation breeds inequalities—but she
is equally wary of a system that doesn't allow people to opt
out of becoming organ donors after death.

"Why make everyone pay a body tax?" she asks. "We have
60 million people who are uninsured in this country; why
should we force the people who we denied health care in their
life to offer up their bodies after they die? The history of
transplants has been replete with doctors who have put them-

selves above the law and (think) that they are ahead of the morality of the time and that society has to catch up with them," she said.

"This proposal doesn't seem to be any different," she added.

If mandatory donation is politically unfeasible now, the United States could consider an opt-out rather than the opt-in organ donation policy, known as "presumed consent" and adopted in various guises in France, Spain, Australia, Belgium and Portugal. (At present, no country mandates that organs must be relinquished at death.)

These laws vary in their details but in general assume that someone would want to be an organ donor unless they explicitly make their objections known by registering in a national online database. Organ donation rates in all of these countries outstrip the U.S. rates. Powerhouse transplant organizations in the Unites States like the American Kidney Fund have lobbied for this system since 2004 but have yet to make headway in national policy.

"Research shows that there would be an increase of between 16 percent to 50 percent in the availability of organs, and others have speculated that this would eliminate the shortage of organs in some categories," said Eric Johnson, professor of business at Columbia University and a proponent of presumed consent policy.

Portugal Has Implemented a Presumed Consent Law

The Portugal News

The Portugal News *is a weekly English-language newspaper in Portugal. In the following viewpoint, the reporter discusses Portugal's presumed consent law, which is considered much more effective in obtaining organs for transplant than an "opt-in" or "registered consent" system. It also has proven to be controversial with many people. One issue of concern in Portugal is the shortage of medical staff, especially surgeons, trained in organ removal, explains the author.*

As you read, consider the following questions:

1. How many organ donations are made in Portugal per every million inhabitants, according to the author?
2. According to 2005 statistics, how many hospitals were equipped to undertake transplants in Portugal?
3. How many transplants were conducted in Portugal in 2005, according to health officials?

It is not a widely known fact, but anyone residing in Portugal, Portuguese or foreign, is presumed a consenting organ donor unless the contrary is manifested by obtaining a legal document that states the person does not want to be consid-

"The Truth Behind Organ Donation in Portugal," *The Portugal News*, July 19, 2008. Reproduced by permission.

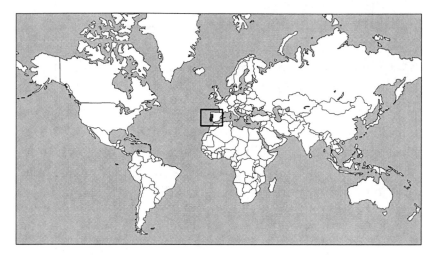

ered for donation upon his or her death. This is the basis of the country's organ donation 'Presumed Consent' law, which whilst not totally mandatory (relatives' consent in many cases is still sought), is believed by numerous researchers to be more effective in saving lives compared with the 'registered consent' system. It is also a topic that has frequently caused turbulent ethical debate.

Portugal's 'Presumed Consent' law is contrary to that of the UK [United Kingdom]. In Britain, a person must manifest their wish to be a donor by registering and carrying a donor's card.

'Presumed Consent' is practised in only a handful of other countries, including France, Spain, Australia and Belgium.

Any national or expatriate with full legal residency in Portugal is subject to this law and seen as a potential and consenting donor if, after a postmortem has been conducted, all the necessary requisites are fulfilled and the person has not officially declared their opposition.

If a person is not willing to be a presumed-consenting donor, there is an option to ensure their rights and wishes are respected.

A Registry for Non-Donors

RENNDA—the national registry for non-donors—was created to be signed by anyone living in Portugal and wanting out of the 'Presumed Consent' law.

This registry also aims to offer more information about donation and transplants in Portugal, as well as an option to those who may be in doubt concerning 'mandatory' organ donation, largely with foreign residents and immigrants in mind who come from countries where mandatory donation is not part of the health system, such as the UK.

In Portugal, potential and presumed donors include victims of untimely death, such as those involved in car accidents and those who are being kept on life support machines after being pronounced clinically dead; those medically classified as brain dead and those who have been autopsied due to a suspicious death but are considered suitable candidates.

Enrolling on the non-donor registry can be done in any health centre across the country, or online. It is effective four days after receiving printed confirmation of enlistment.

In Portugal, potential and presumed donors include victims of untimely death, such as those involved in car accidents and those who are being kept on life support machines after being pronounced clinically dead; those medically classified as brain dead and those who have been autopsied due to a suspicious death but are considered suitable candidates.

Routine health exams are carried out to assess their eligibility, which once verified, and with the family's consent, the organ is removed by the hospital or, if the hospital does not have a specifically trained team (as is the case at Portimão's CHBA Barlavento Hospital), a specialist medical team is urgently dispatched to intervene and remove the organ.

Viable recipients are then contacted through the Portuguese transplant association and given one hour to deliberate, and either accept or refuse.

The recipient must then make their way to the hospital where the transplant will take place in as short a time as possible.

Britain vs. Portugal

In 2005, 6298 patients in Britain were waiting for organ transplants, including 5502 waiting for kidney transplants, for which there is an average waiting period of 729 days. Surveys show that around 90 per cent of the UK population would be willing to donate organs after death, though only 12.5 million, around 21 per cent of the UK population, were on the NHS [National Health Service] organ donor register that year.

In Portugal, 2004 was one of the country's best years for obtaining organs, taking third place amongst other EU [European Union] countries and is also one of the European countries where most transplants take place.

However, figures have since fallen and currently only 18 organs are gained from every million inhabitants.

The issue of transplants in Portugal was again recently thrust into the limelight when Prime Minister José Sócrates' brother went to Spain to receive a lung transplant, an organ for which there is a great shortage in Portugal.

So far this year [2008], two lung transplants have taken place here, though it is estimated an average 15–20 lung transplants are needed annually; a demand that is clearly not being satisfied.

Only one hospital in Portugal—Hospital [de] Santa Marta—undertakes this complex procedure.

Figures show that in 2005, 22 hospitals were equipped to undertake transplants, the majority in Lisbon, at least six in northern Portugal, two in Madeira/Porto Santo, and none in southern Portugal.

That same year, 1432 transplants were conducted, including kidney, liver, heart, pancreas, lung, cornea and bone marrow transplants, extracted from 232 donors at 37 hospitals around the country.

Growing waiting lists and the unpredictability of when a suitable candidate will emerge further complicate the matter.

CHBA

In 2004, Portimão's Barlavento Hospital (CHBA) was the only hospital not to register any donors; a year later, it supplied only one organ.

Nonetheless, the hospital says it has all the facilities to keep potential donors in prime condition until a specialist team of surgeons . . . arrives from Lisbon, bringing with them all the necessary preservation and travel equipment.

CHBA does not have trained specialists to carry out organ removal, though it is an area that is being looked into.

According to the hospital's clinical director, Dr. Pedro Quaresma, "It is not lack of funding that has prevented this from happening before now, but lack of staff time, as there are only a handful of surgeons who could be trained in this specialist area and volunteering their time that is already overstretched, is a problem".

Dr. Quaresma told the *Portugal News* he believes that, "given the size of Portugal and its population, there is no need for transplants to be undertaken in the Algarve, nor is there a demand".

He explained that the law concerning transplants in Portugal is currently experiencing a shake-up, and is in revision. A recent law change has allowed the transplanting of organs from live donors, which until recently was not permitted.

However, few transplants have been carried out from live donors as in many cases extensive psychological exams, match probability and other health tests of both willing donors and recipients make the procedure an arduous affair.

Last year, Portuguese organ transplant doctors and specialists received 23 million euros in incentives, culminating in 1330 transplants, which is less than the disappointing total recorded in 2005.

Periodical and Internet Sources Bibliography

The following articles have been selected to supplement the diverse views presented in this chapter.

CNN.com
"China Hopes Organ Donor System Stops Trafficking," August 26, 2009. www.cnn.com.

Michael Cook
"Recycling Euthanasia Organs in Belgium," *Crisis Magazine*, June 20, 2011.

Globe & Mail
"How Making Organ Donation Easier Can Save Lives," June 15, 2011.

John Harris
"We Have an Organ Donation Crisis, So Pay People to Give," *Times* (London), January 31, 2012.

IRIN
"Egypt: Controversial Organ Transplant Bill Welcomed by WHO," February 7, 2010. www .irinnews.org.

Olivia Olarte
"Organ Transplants May Start by 2012," *Khaleej Times*, November 23, 2011.

Betsan Powys
"Is Death Devolved? Let Me Know," BBC News, January 12, 2012. www.bbc.co.uk.

Catherine Rampell
"How Can Countries Encourage Organ Donation?," *New York Times*, December 22, 2009.

Peter Ritter
"Legalizing the Organ Trade?," *Time*, August 19, 2008.

Ian Sample
"Organ Donors Could Get Rewards," *Guardian*, April 19, 2010.

Christopher Watson
"Transplants Are Cost Effective and Life Changing," *Times* (London), January 30, 2012.

CHAPTER 4

The Problem of Organ Trafficking

Organ Trafficking Is a Global Problem

Ami Cholia

Ami Cholia is a contributor to the Huffington Post. *In the following viewpoint, she claims that recent cases of American politicians charged with organ trafficking bring to the forefront the global nature of the problem. Cholia maintains that the illegal kidney trade has skyrocketed in the past few decades, leading to poor people in a number of countries selling their organs and in some cases resorting to stealing organs from cadavers to meet the growing need. Cholia further explains that corruption and exploitation are also issues that have added to the organ trafficking industry.*

As you read, consider the following questions:

1. According to Nancy Scheper-Hughes, how many trafficked kidneys are there every year?
2. How much does a seller earn for a kidney on average, according to Cholia?
3. What country is the only one where the practice of selling a kidney for profit is legal?

Ami Cholia, "Illegal Organ Trafficking Poses a Global Problem," *Huffington Post*, July 25, 2009. Copyright © 2012 AOL Inc. Used with permission.

The recent New Jersey corruption probe, which resulted in the arrest of 44 people including state legislators, government officials and several rabbis for running an international money laundering racket that trafficked human organs, has brought Israel into the spotlight for organ transplants. Despite some growing awareness, the international organ trade industry is not well understood due to lack of information and the widespread nature of the problem.

A Global Problem

According to the World Health Organization (WHO), the search for organs has intensified around the world because of an increase in kidney diseases and not enough available kidneys. Only 10 percent of the estimated need was met in 2005. As a result, the illegal kidney trade has increased tremendously over the past couple of years with the extent of illegal kidney transplants unknown even to the WHO.

Nancy Scheper-Hughes, founding director of Organs Watch, an academic research project that deals with organ transplants at the University of California [UC], Berkeley, has said that a conservative estimate would put the number of trafficked kidneys at 15,000 each year.

Poverty and corruption are underlying themes behind sellers giving up their organs as most donors see it as the only option to make money.

Outside of Israel, Egypt, Brazil, South Africa, Indonesia, India and Iraq are some of the biggest players in the game. Organ trafficking is illegal in all these countries. The seller generally earns between $2,000 to $6,000 for a kidney, though post-operation care is almost never taken into account. Unaware of all the risks involved, the donors often find themselves even worse off than before the operation, and with little or no money left to help them live.

"Kid selling his Dad's organs to a mafia boss on the internet," cartoon by Geoff Purvis, www.CartoonStock.com. Copyright © Geoff Purvis. Reproduction rights obtainable from www.CartoonStock.com.

Poverty and corruption are underlying themes behind sellers giving up their organs as most donors see it as the only option to make money. For most buyers, who have been waiting on transplant lists for months, desperate need and frustration push them to commit the illegal act. Often, they are told that the men and women they are buying the kidneys from are perfectly healthy and in good shape.

A Desperate Act

In some parts of India, poor people use their kidneys as collateral for money lenders. Lawrence Cohen, UC Berkeley professor of anthropology, has documented that the kidneys in the region are often sold to the wealthy in Sri Lanka, Bangladesh, the Gulf states, the United Kingdom and the United States.

Cohen, in a press release published by UC Berkeley, states that while most people sold their kidneys to get out of debt, they were back in debt very shortly.

> "Most sellers would say, 'I'd do it again. I have a family to support. What choice did I have?'" said Cohen.

> In some neighborhoods, the structure of debt appeared to rest on kidney selling, since lenders would advance money knowing the organs were collateral.

> But I argue that the money from kidneys didn't really get these families out of debt. Moreover, there was no follow-up care after the operation, nor efforts to prevent infection in the donor.

> Nor was there a clear benefit for the recipient, due to the high cost of being maintained on cyclosporine, a drug that suppresses immune reactions to transplants. People were not informed about the cost of the maintenance drugs, and middle-class recipients could find themselves deeply in debt after the operation, said Cohen.

In places like Egypt, which the WHO has declared as an organ-trafficking hot spot, this ABC report tells of a similar problem:

> For years, word has spread among Egypt's destitute that selling a kidney—sometimes for as little as $2,000—can be a quick way out of a debt or to keep from sinking deeper into poverty. At rundown cafes, they are hunted by middlemen

working for labs that match donors and recipients, many of whom are foreigners drawn to Egypt's thriving, underground organ trade.

In Brazil the situation is more complicated than a simple give-and-take performed for large sums of money, according to Scheper-Hughes in an interview with Threemonkeysonline .com.

> [She said that in Brazil she found] softer forms of sale that raised serious questions about the exploitation of people in subordinate work positions. Exchanges were taking place between employers and employees or wealthy people and their domestic workers in which the lower status individuals "donated" their kidneys in return for secure employment, housing or other basic needs. Scheper-Hughes also is investigating the allegations of two women in São Paulo who woke up from gynecological surgery without a kidney.

She also found widespread abuse of the cadavers of poor people, involving eyes, pineal glands and heart valves in Brazil and South Africa.

In Iraq, where unemployment is at least 18 percent, people sell their organs to survive much like in the rest of the organ trade hot spots.

According to an Al Jazeera report:

> The capital Baghdad is somewhat of a central hub for the trade, with hundreds of people estimated to have sold organs such as their kidneys to dealers who then sell them for massive profits to desperately ill people willing to pay.

Iran, on the other hand, is the only country where the practice of selling one's kidney for profit is legal. The Charity Association for the Support of Kidney Patients (CASKP) and the Charity Foundation for Special Diseases (CFSD) control the trade of organs with the support of the government, and the country has no wait lists for kidney transplantation.

Nepal's Illegal Organ Trade Is on the Rise

Tara Bhattarai

Tara Bhattarai is reporter for the Global Press Institute. In the following viewpoint, she investigates the booming market for illegally obtained organs, especially kidneys, in Nepal. Bhattarai reports that unscrupulous agents recruit poor and vulnerable men and women to donate their kidneys on the black market, and it is suspected that hundreds of thousands of Nepali have sold their kidneys this way. Although there is a law in place against organ trafficking in Nepal, Bhattarai finds that law enforcement has been lax in this area for years.

As you read, consider the following questions:

1. What explanation does the author give for the lack of information on the organ black market in Nepal?

2. According to Rajya Laxmi Koirala, how many Nepali have sold a kidney during the last decade?

3. What does the author say is the punishment for criminals found to be selling human organs or aiding in this activity in Nepal?

Tara Bhattarai, "Illegal Organ Trade on the Rise in Nepal," Global Press Institute, March 22, 2010. Copyright © 2010 by the Global Press Institute. All rights reserved. Reproduced by permission.

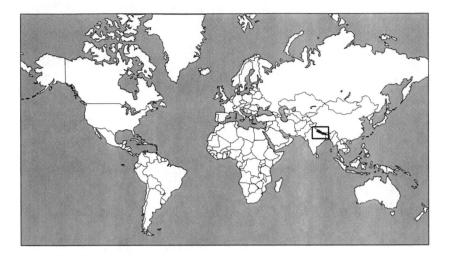

A thick fog envelops the hilly areas of Kavrepalanchok, a central district, widely known as Kavre. This rural village is situated 55 kilometers east of Nepal's capital, Kathmandu. Passenger buses and trucks heading to Tatopani, a trading hub near the Chinese border along the Araniko Highway, struggle to negotiate blind turns. Visibility is low. Near the highway, Sambar Tamang, 49 of Hokse village, is unfazed by the honking buses moving by at a snail's pace.

He basks in the sunlight in the courtyard where his four grandchildren are playing, braving the chilly weather. The sunlight fails to warm Tamang's spirits as he sits near a bonfire, brooding.

Tamang's Story

"I desperately want to work, but my health prohibits me," says Tamang, as he watches the children play. At 49 years old, he is a skinny and lanky man. He risked his life to become the owner of a one-story thatched house—built of the local red clay and stone boulders, the roof is made of old tin sheets. There is just one room, which is used for lodging, cooking and all domestic purposes.

Three years ago, Tamang had nothing but a piece of land. He lived in a hut in the village with four children and his hearing-impaired wife, whom he married after his first wife died of malnutrition in 1994.

"I often used to dream of becoming the owner of a house one day in my life," he says. To follow his dream, Tamang took out a loan from a local merchant and built a medium-sized house.

No sooner had he bought the house than he was pressured to pay back the loan, which amounted to 25,000 rupees ($330 USD). He had pledged to return this money at any cost within four years. Tamang had been paying 700 rupees as interest every month from the daily wage of 200 rupees ($2.60) he earned as a porter in Kathmandu, where he spent over a week each month. "Repaying the huge amount of [the] loan within the maturity period was like a hard nut to crack," he says. "So I went to Kathmandu one month [after] the house construction was over hoping that I could make money for it."

This went on for three years. Finally, one day, he met three people who assured him that they would turn his dream into reality—they would help him pay off his home loan. Tamang says he was willing to do anything to earn the money to pay back the loan. The group he met in Kathmandu was in a black market trade. Later, he learned, their trade was human organs.

"I was lured with money to sell one of my kidneys," he admits. Since Tamang was feeling the burden of debt, he agreed. "I sold my right kidney for 50,000 rupees." For about $650 USD, Tamang underwent a dangerous operation that left him with a deep scar, long-term health problems and only one kidney.

A Booming Black Market Business

Just like Tamang, many people have a similar story to tell. In Hokse and the neighboring villages, local residents estimate nearly 100 people have sold kidneys on the black market. The total number of individuals who have sold kidneys in Nepal is unknown; although many say this black market business is thriving. There are still no nongovernmental organizations working against the organ-selling business. Police say they do not have exact records of kidney agents or sellers.

"In the marginalized settlements of Kavre and its neighboring district Sindhupalchok, many people are living with one kidney," says social worker Uddhav Hamal of Singapur village. "My 40-year-old neighbor [Krishna Sahi] went to India six months ago and sold her left kidney. Just a month ago, she died after her right kidney ceased to function."

"In this village five people have already died," Hamal confirms. "We stopped some villagers from going to India, but some still sold their kidneys secretly."

Tamang had a tough time working in Kathmandu. "I could not earn [enough] to feed my family, even working for 18 hours a day," he says. "When I was approached by a kidney agent to sell my kidney, I was startled in the beginning. But later I gave in to his offer of 50,000 rupees."

The agent took the illiterate man to the Indian city of Siliguri with Tamang's consent. They boarded a train and got off at an unknown place, which Tamang says he could not make out. "He took me to a hospital there," he says.

On the very first day of his admission at the hospital, Tamang had his blood tested. "Then I was kept at the [hospital] for 19 days. The agent told me I have to sit in the hospital for at least two weeks. But I don't know why," says Tamang.

After 20 days, his turn finally came and his right kidney was removed by the Indian doctors. "After [the] operation I thought I was dying for a while, but the greed of [the] much-needed 50,000 rupees didn't let me feel the pain," he says. "Three days later I returned to Kathmandu with [a] fresh wound."

Upon reaching home, Tamang realized that his decision to sell his kidney was a mistake because he could no longer work in the field or the house like he used to do. "I am weak and fall ill constantly now. I cannot control [urine]," he says of his newly developed incontinence. "Doing heavy work is out of my thinking nowadays."

Tamang's youngest daughter was also approached by the kidney agents, but luckily for her, the blood test showed that she didn't have enough hemoglobin in her blood and was declared unfit for organ donation.

Kavrepalanchok is a hotbed of the kidney trade, says Deepak Adhikari, a local reporter of *Kantipur Daily*, Nepal's largest newspaper. "In the past five years, kidney sales have gone up significantly," says Adhikari who suspects hundreds of thousands of Nepali people have sold their kidneys.

The investigative department of the police department here [in Kathmandu] is aware of many active kidney agents baiting rural villagers with the promise of money if they travel to India to sell a kidney.

Sociologist Rajya Laxmi Koirala claims more than 100,000 Nepalis have sold a kidney during the last decade. Due to economic hardship, lack of awareness and the seemingly "easy money," she says many poor Nepali people are lured to India to sell their kidneys. "I have seen Nepali students in India selling their kidneys to pay their tuition fees," Koirala adds.

Organ Agents Thrive in Urban Kathmandu

Adhikari says about a dozen kidney agents are known to be active in Kathmandu and police statistics agree with this figure. The investigative department of the police department here is aware of many active kidney agents baiting rural villagers with the promise of money if they travel to India to sell a kidney.

The growing kidney trade in Nepal came to light on February 5, 2008, when wanted Indian kidney kingpin, Amit Kumar, was arrested in southern Nepal near India. Kumar had been hiding there since his clinic in Gurgaon, India, was raided by police earlier in the year.

Kumar was, according to police, behind 600 illegal kidney transplants. He and his associates obtained kidneys illegally from poor people in Nepal, then transplanted them to needy patients who could pay exorbitant rates. The normal cost of a renal transplant is around 300,000 rupees ($4,000) in India. However police suspect around half a dozen kidney agents serve clients from the U.S., U.K., Canada, Saudi Arabia and other countries. "These agents even charge up to one million rupees ($13,000) from rich clients," says Adhikari.

Doctors and lawyers argue that the illegal organ trade is flourishing in Nepal because of the demand from rich patients suffering from renal failure in Europe, Canada and the United States.

Government Remains Motionless

Nepal's law considers the sale of human organs a crime based on the Human Trafficking (Control) Act and the Human Organ Transplant Act, says lawyer Dilli Ram Mainali. "The Human Organ Transplant Act prohibits conducting the transplant-related activities without prior licensing from the concerned authority," says Mainali. "[The] Human Trafficking Act considers illegal organ transplant as an act punishable as trafficking of [a] human being."

Those found to be selling human organs or aiding in this activity face a jail sentence up to 10 years and a fine of 500,000 rupees ($6,500), Mainali adds.

However, poor implementation of the law is taking its toll, he says, adding, "The government should tighten the rules if the kidney agents [are] to be reined in."

Though the law allows only a blood relative to donate a kidney to ailing kin, kidney brokers exploit the poor by making false documents, says senior kidney specialist Dr. Rishi Kumar Kafle.

"We have repeatedly informed government authorities to control this unscrupulous act, but they are still silent on this matter," he says.

A Skyrocketing Demand

Doctors and lawyers argue that the illegal organ trade is flourishing in Nepal because of the demand from rich patients suffering from renal failure in Europe, Canada and the United States. Other developing nations are also known to battle with the illegal trade of human organs.

"As long as the demand stays, the supply will continue," says Koirala. "And the legislation designed to prevent it is failing."

"We are well aware of this thriving illegal [act]. Thus, we have instructed police to take stern action against them," says Home [Affairs] Minister Bhim Rawal. However, the police have yet to make a single arrest.

"Kidney victims lodge complaints at police offices against the agents," says police officer Dirgha Bogati. "There were two cases related to illegal [sale] of [a] kidney, but police could not move to court due to lack of necessary documents and evidence."

VIEWPOINT 3

India's Organ Trade Exploits the Country's Most Vulnerable People

Thomas Schmitt

Thomas Schmitt is a journalist. In the following viewpoint, he explores organ trafficking in India that involves ruthless agents exploiting desperately poor young women and men from the worst slums in the country. Schmitt points out that many of these donors only make enough money to pay off their debts, and they often fall right back into financial problems. Despite steps to curb the practice, crafty criminals and corruptible state employees and doctors have allowed the practice to flourish. Another problem, says Schmitt, is that the police have failed to investigate the crime in many areas.

As you read, consider the following questions:

1. According to Schmitt, what is the nickname of Villi-vakkam, a slum in the north of Chennai in India?

2. How many Indians require a kidney transplant every year, according to estimates?

3. According to Thiru V.K. Subburaj, what percentage of organ donors in India live below the poverty line?

Thomas Schmitt, "Organ Trade Thrives in Indian Slums," *Der Spiegel*, June 15, 2007. Copyright © 2007 by the New York Times Syndicate. All rights reserved. Reproduced by permission.

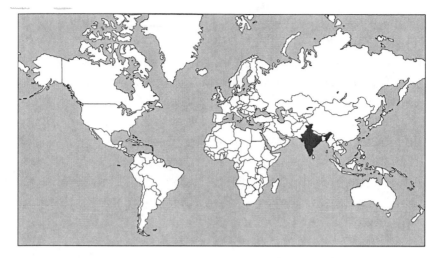

The note is attached to a tree trunk across from the central hospital in Chennai (formerly Madras), a major city in southern India. Written in scrawly handwriting, the note advertizes its author's "top notch kidney" for 30,000 rupees, the equivalent of €500 ($664). Asked about his offer, the vendor—a 30-year-old Tamil—says "no middleman" is involved in the deal. He adds that he urgently needs the money to "pay back debts."

This offer is no isolated case in Chennai. On the contrary: The metropolis of around 7 million people has the questionable reputation of being the main trafficking hub for the organ trade in India. And the items for sale are mainly kidneys. After all, every human being has two of those and can get by with just one if need be.

Sometimes the trade takes on a bizarre character. Villivakkam, a slum in the north of Chennai, is known as "Kidneyvakkam" or "Kidneytown" among the locals. Surveys conducted for the health ministry show almost every family includes someone who has sold their kidney. The situation is similar in the neighboring refugee camp of Tsunami Nagar, which was set up for the victims of the 2004 Indian Ocean

177

tsunami. Here, the kidneys of patients in good health can be bought "for between 20,000 and 40,000 rupees," one former middleman reveals.

"The kidney donors are often poor young women," reports George Kurian from the Christian Medical College [and] Hospital in Vellore. "The buyers, on the other hand, are usually older and well-off men." According to press reports, about 100,000 Indians require a kidney transplant every year. In addition, some two million suffer from serious kidney problems. The demand is huge—and the kidneys tend to go to those with the most money.

Money Lenders, Middlemen and Corrupt Officials

The Indian government already tried to pass a law regulating the removal and donation of kidneys as early as 1994. But the government could not put a stop to the illegal trade, since the law allows people to donate their organs to complete strangers, provided they are in some sort of "relationship"—no matter of what kind—with the interested party.

It is impossible to prevent money changing hands under the counter, even though, theoretically, every transplant needs to be approved by a handpicked panel of doctors and other experts. But the dramatic increase in demand for kidneys leads to more and more organ donations being approved despite the absence of conclusive proof that the transaction really is a noncommercial "donation." "We know an organized organ trade exists," says C. Ravindranath, the former chairman of the authorization committee. "It's just that we can't prove it."

Jogesh Amalorpavanathan, the organ transplant coordinator at the public central hospital in Chennai, is only too familiar with the situation. He explains that the illegal organ trade only works because of the well-rehearsed cooperation between crafty money lenders, dubious middlemen and corruptible state employees. The latter provide the counterfeit proof of identity, while the middlemen are responsible for "customer contact" and the money lenders for the financial settlement, according to Amalorpavanathan.

The Indian government already tried to pass a law regulating the removal and donation of kidneys as early as 1994.

Health Risks

The issue has been hotly debated in the press, prompting the government of the state of Tamil Nadu to order an investigation. But the police unit charged with fighting crime promptly refused to investigate, arguing that only the authorization committee has a mandate to look into irregularities in the organ trade. The only response to that explanation from those involved in the trade is a tired smile: Now they can go about their business as usual.

And kidneys are in ample supply: Sums of between €500 and €700 are no trifle in India, and there is a correspondingly large number of people willing to surrender a kidney. But in the long term, the organ vendors don't benefit. A study by the health ministry shows that the organ transplants are associated with enormous health risks. Moreover, they don't even improve the donors' financial situation in the long term.

"Ninety percent of the organ donors live below the poverty line," says health expert Thiru V.K. Subburaj. "But by the time their debts have been paid off and enough food and clothing has been bought for the family, most of the money has been used up."

Kidney Exports

But that isn't all. Many organ donors complain about having received too little aftercare and admit that they were left in a weakened state for a long time after the operation. They are no longer able to perform their everyday work as usual. This leads to the follow-up health costs being much higher, in the long run, than the financial benefits associated with the organ sale. It's not even unusual for the donors to "die from the effects of a negligently carried out operation," says Ravindranath from the authorization committee.

But the organ recipients wash their hands of this murky trade. Barely 3 percent of those questioned for a survey admitted to ever having heard about the lucrative trade that prospers off the backs of the poorest of the poor.

The media had hoped a recent conference in Chennai could provide a solution. But the debate between the experts was sobering. Tamil Nadu's health minister Thiru Ramachandran repeatedly called for more controls—but these calls fell on deaf ears. On the contrary: Most of the 50 participants went so far as to call for a complete liberalization of the organ trade. "If the wealthy can buy anything they want with their money, then why shouldn't they be able to buy human organs as well?" one participant asked.

Meanwhile, the organ trade has developed into a veritable export industry. Every year more than 1,000 kidneys from India go abroad—most of them to Arab countries—even though the domestic demand is far from having been met. Given such demand, it's unlikely that the sordid business is going to end anytime soon.

Egypt's Illegal Organ Trafficking Endangers the Poor

Theodore May

Theodore May is a journalist. In the following viewpoint, he reports that Egyptian authorities have seen a troubling rise in organ trafficking in the past few years. May attributes the booming market in human organs to the country's stifling poverty and to unscrupulous agents that prey on Egypt's poor. Donors are lured by money but are often mistreated and deprived of adequate aftercare that threatens their lives. May explains that to combat the growing problem, the Egyptian Parliament is considering a law to better regulate organ transplants in the country and make organs more readily available at government hospitals.

As you read, consider the following questions:

1. According to May, what percentage of Egyptians live on $2 or less a day?

2. Who are seeking organs on the black market, according to the viewpoint?

3. Since the passage of the new law in 2001, how many kidney transplants do government hospitals perform on average in Egypt?

Theodore May, "Organ Trade Endangers Egypt's Poorest," *Global Post*, April 8, 2009. Copyright © 2009 by Global News Enterprises. All rights reserved. Reproduced by permission.

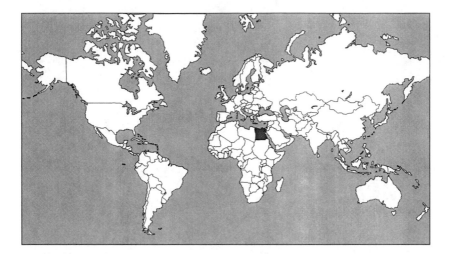

Kidneys are in high demand. Livers—or part thereof—too. So much so that each organ can fetch a couple of thousands of dollars on the black market.

At those prices, one would guess that we are not talking the bovine, ovine, or poultry variety.

Yes, add to Egypt's myriad social problems rampant trafficking in human organs for the purpose of medical transplants.

A Booming Market

Egyptian authorities have seen a rise in this lucrative trade over the past several years and only now believe they are beginning to get control of the problem. The problem is symptomatic of Egypt's extreme poverty.

The price tag on a kidney or part of a liver comes to just a couple thousand dollars, a small fee considering the risks involved. But in a country where 40 percent of the population lives on $2 or less a day, to the most destitute here it's more money than they may make over the course of several years.

Most of those seeking organs on the black market are Arabs from the region, according to the ministry of health. They connect with traffickers who, in turn, source donors from among Egypt's poorest citizens.

The ministry first caught wind of the problem in 2006 when a small number of cases were reported to the authorities. The ministry, working with the country's security forces, launched a series of raids on suspected clinics and made a number of arrests.

The unintended consequence of this, however, was to drive the organ trade further underground, which dramatically increased the risk to the patients.

"What we came to as a conclusion: those who used to use hostels in Mohandiseen and Dokki [two central commercial districts in Cairo], then moved their operations underground," said a ministry of health spokesman, Dr. Abdel Rahman Shahin. "This means more danger for the patient."

Egyptian authorities have seen a rise in this lucrative trade over the past several years and only now believe they are beginning to get control of the problem. The problem is symptomatic of Egypt's extreme poverty.

Cruel Practices

Routinely, patients were taken from illegal clinics while still unconscious because the doctors feared getting caught. In some cases patients were dumped back on the street before waking up.

Dr. Adel Hosny, head of liver transplants at Cairo's Kasr El Aini Hospital, concurred that doctors in illegal clinics often discharged organ donors long before they should. He said that patients need to be in intensive care for at least 12 hours after liver surgery.

Infection was another big risk in the illegal clinics, Hosny said, because there is no way to guarantee the sterility of the operating room.

Egypt and Organ Trafficking

The World Health Organization (WHO) has identified Egypt as one of five organ trafficking hot spots. Over 95 percent of all kidney transplants, and at least 30 percent of all partial liver transplants, are between nonrelated donors and recipients—which experts say is a strong indication that a payment is involved.

Cam McGrath, "Move to End Organ Trafficking,"
Inter Press Service, May 18, 2009. http://ipsnews.net.

While organ trafficking has been driven deeper underground, some have begun making more brazen public efforts to buy and sell organs. "People have begun showing up at hospitals with a family member . . . doctors only find out later that they weren't family," Hosny said.

A New Law

To combat commercial organ sales, the Egyptian Parliament is set to consider a new law that will raise the bar on donors to prove that transplant isn't a commercial venture. At the same time, the law will make more organs readily available through government hospitals.

This legislation, said Shahin, may finally slow the organ trade business in Egypt, which has become one of the biggest markets for the illicit trade of organs. China and Pakistan lead the world, according to the Albany, New York-based Institute for Humanist Studies.

"The regulations are very clear," Shahin said. "They have to get permission from the medical syndicate. They have to be blood relatives, and if they are not blood relatives, they must appear in front of a committee and prove there is no commercial element."

This process for gaining approval isn't new in Egypt, but the proposed law will toughen enforcement standards. The number of legal transplants in the country is still low in relation to demand.

Government hospitals have reportedly performed 350 partial liver transplants since they were made legal in 2001, 400 bone marrow transplants over the past three years, and 60 to 80 kidney transplants a year.

Other Measures and Controversies

In another effort to reduce the need for the underground trade, the government is trying to loosen standards on who qualifies as an organ donor, hopefully boosting the number of transplants by increasing the availability of organs.

But as lawmakers debate how best to do this, they have clashed with members of Egypt's religious establishment and set off a hot debate in the country that centers on the very definition of death.

"You have two types of death," Hosny said, "the brain death, when the person still has a beating heart. Then there is the death when the heart is not beating anymore. This is where the debate lies."

Politicians are still haggling over the definition of death with leading religious scholars—among them Sheikh Muhammad Sayyid Tantawi, who runs Al-Azhar Mosque, and Ali Gomaa, Grand Mufti of Egypt. The two are considered to be Egypt's most influential clerics.

The other controversy surrounds the use of organs from executed criminals. Though it is unclear how many executions take place in Egypt each year, legalizing the use of a convict's organs, with or without their consent, would seriously boost supply on the legal market, Shahin said. Several religious clerics have recently spoken out in favor of the measure.

"They are saying that when [convicts'] organs are taken, they're compensating for the bad they did," said Shahin, paraphrasing some in the religious establishment.

While the new transplant law still hangs in limbo, many medical officials are hoping for any measure that would make transplants more readily available and thus deal a blow to the illegal trade.

Kosovo Is Rocked by an Organ Trafficking Scandal

T.J.

T.J. is a journalist and blogger at the Economist. *In the following viewpoint, T.J. investigates allegations against high-ranking authorities in Kosovo, including Prime Minister Hashim Thaçi, in kidnapping, murder, and organ trafficking after the 1999 Kosovo war. T.J. asserts evidence and witness statements corroborate the charges, which some people believe were never really fully investigated by international authorities like the United Nations, who it is thought covered up the crimes in order to move forward. T.J. urges a legitimate and thorough criminal investigation by credible authorities in order to uncover the truth and finally prosecute any criminal wrongdoing.*

As you read, consider the following questions:

1. According to the author, how many individuals were kidnapped and killed—some of them for their organs—by criminals close to the Kosovo prime minister?
2. Where do witnesses say that these killings took place?
3. When do the witnesses say that the crimes took place, according to witness statements?

T.J., "Is the Mud Sticking?," *Eastern Approaches* (blog), *The Economist*, February 24, 2011. Copyright © 2011 by The Economist. All rights reserved. Reproduced by permission.

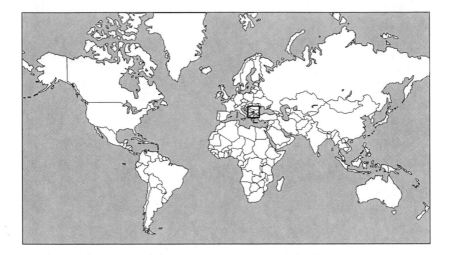

Kosovo marked the third anniversary of its independence on February 17th [2011] in sombre mood. Only last July the country's leaders were riding high ... in the wake of an advisory opinion by the International Court of Justice that its declaration of independence had not been illegal. Now their reputations are in tatters.

First came allegations of fraud in last December's elections, which angered its strongest supporter, the United States. Soon afterwards, a report produced by Dick Marty, a Swiss politician and former prosecutor, made lurid claims about the involvement of Kosovo's leadership in organized crime. In the last few days two new documents have come to light that appear to bolster the most nightmarish of those allegations.

First, a disclaimer. In Balkan politics, the dictum, "if you are not with us, you are against us" usually applies. Some readers have attacked this blog simply for reporting on the Marty affair. As a fog of confusion, claims and counterclaims swirl over the allegations laid against Kosovo's leaders, we lay out here what is already known about the issue, and what is new.

The Allegations

Last December, Mr Marty delivered a report to the Council of Europe that alleged that Hashim Thaçi, who has just begun a second term as Kosovo's prime minister, was close to people who, after the 1999 Kosovo war, had kidnapped some 500 Serbs, Albanians and others, all of whom were eventually killed. Some of them, the report claimed, were murdered so that their organs could be harvested and sold. Mr Thaçi has vigorously denied the claims.

Mr Marty's allegations were not new. Their first public outing was in a 2008 book by Carla Del Ponte, the former prosecutor of the UN [United Nations] war crimes [International Criminal] Tribunal for the Former Yugoslavia in the Hague (ICTY), and Chuck Sudetic, a former ICTY analyst.

Now, however, documents have been leaked to the Serbian press that appear to strengthen Mr Marty's claims. They contain transcripts of original interviews with witnesses gathered by a key source known to me and handed over confidentially in 2003 to the then UN administration in Kosovo (UNMIK [United Nations Interim Administration Mission in Kosovo]). The witnesses in the documents are quoted as saying they believed kidnapped Serbs and others had been killed for their organs.

At the time there was no corroboration for these claims. But they did inspire UNMIK investigators and a team from the ICTY to visit, in February 2004, the now-infamous "yellow house" in rural north Albania, near the town of Burrel, where the witnesses said the killings had taken place.

A forensic report produced by UNMIK says that the team found traces of blood at the yellow house, but that these did not constitute "conclusive evidence" of criminal acts. Neither ICTY nor UNMIK undertook a search for bodies, and no full criminal investigation was ever undertaken. Yet the traces, as well as medical paraphernalia found outside the house, could have been considered to be corroborative physical evidence of the claims made in the witness statements we now know about.

The Politics of Organ Trafficking

Why did UNMIK shelve the case? Political expediency, basically. It had to work with the men implicated by the witnesses on a daily basis. The implications of what a criminal investigation might uncover horrified those in the UN charged with building a modern and stable administration in the post-war territory.

As for the ICTY, its prosecutors concluded that, even if crimes had been committed, they were beyond their jurisdiction because they had taken place after the Kosovo war had ended. Several years later, in a mysterious and embarrassing move for which it has never been properly taken to task, the ICTY destroyed the physical evidence collected at the yellow house. Had it been kept it might have yielded the DNA samples critical for a full criminal investigation.

The implications of what a criminal investigation might uncover horrified those in the UN charged with building a modern and stable administration in the post-war territory.

As Mr Sudetic notes, because neither UNMIK nor the ICTY pursued the case, they were able to claim that they had no evidence to support the allegations. This was not, however, the case for Mr Marty, who conducted a much more thorough investigation. Albanians and others say that Mr Marty was opposed to Kosovo's declaration of independence and claim his report is part of a campaign to smear the new state.

Mr Marty has also been attacked for not revealing details about his sources. He says their lives would be in danger if their identities were known. How convenient, retort the sceptics.

Hashim Thaçi: "The Snake"

Hashim Thaçi was born in 1968, one of nine children born in a farming family in the Drenica region of Kosovo. As a young student, he left the area to study in Pristina, where he was a university student–movement leader. He first tasted politics at this time through his association with a radical Marxist-Leninist group with ties to Albanian dictator Enver Hoxha. . . .

Tired of university politics, he joined forces with Lëvizja Popullore E Kosovës (LPK) leaders and founded an armed movement, which eventually became the Kosovo Liberation Army (KLA). He was expelled from Pristina University and returned to the Drenica region where he joined a movement to agitate Kosovar Albanians. In June 1993, he turned to military action. With two comrades, . . . he launched one of the first armed attacks against Serbian forces. For his terrorist offences he was sentenced, in absentia, to 22 years in prison. He then fled to Luzern and Zurich where he completed his postgraduate studies in political science. He continued his militant activities and by 1997, Thaçi was a leader in a divergent guerilla force.

Thaçi's successes were due in large part to his reputation for violence and ruthlessness. It is not without cause that he has been nicknamed the "Snake." His detractors believe that anyone suspected of being a traitor was viciously mistreated. . . . When questioned, Thaçi avoids answering charges that the KLA engaged in any form of ethnic cleansing or reprisal attacks on Serbians. Thaçi blames anarchists for attempting to create chaos as the new government is formed, but flatly denies any attempts to expel Serbs.

"Hashim Thaçi,"
Gale Biography in Context, January 2012.
http://ic.galegroup.com.

The New Evidence

But the new documents will dismay Mr Marty's critics. They make for sickening reading about what happened in Albania after the war (although it is important to acknowledge that the claims they contain have never been tested by a proper criminal investigation). They also include details of the witnesses' identities, although not their names.

The first document is dated October 30th 2003. It is an internal ICTY text containing an annex with the witness statements gathered by the external source that had been sent to it by UNMIK. The second, dated December 12th 2003, is from the director of UNMIK's department of justice.

A summary of the witness statements in the first document states that between June and October 1999, 100–300 people, mostly Serb men, were abducted and taken to Albania. Between 24 and 100 of them were then taken to secondary detention centres, from where they were moved again to a "makeshift clinic" where "medical equipment and personnel were used to extract body organs from the captives, who then died." The organs were then taken to Tirana airport and flown to Turkey and other destinations.

The document states that the witnesses were all ethnic Albanians who had served in the Kosovo Liberation Army (KLA). Four of them had been involved in the transport of at least 90 Serbs to central and northern Albania. Three of them delivered captives to the "house/clinic" near Burrel (the yellow house), the document states, two of them said they had helped dispose of human remains near the house, and one said he delivered body parts to Tirana airport.

The document also notes that none of the sources claimed to have witnessed the medical procedures. But they all claim that the operations and the transport of body parts took place with at least the knowledge, and in some cases the active involvement, of mid- to senior-level KLA officers.

At one point, the document quotes the sources as saying that: "The operation was supported by men with links to Albanian secret police operatives of the former government of Sali Berisha." Mr Berisha is, again, Albania's prime minister today.

The Names

Significantly, the new documents do not mention Mr Thaçi's name. But they mention Ramush Haradinaj and his brother Daut. Mr Haradinaj is a former KLA commander and prime minister of Kosovo. In 2008 he was acquitted of war crimes by the ICTY, but he is now being retried on some counts after the prosecution successfully alleged witness intimidation.

Mr Haradinaj is a political foe of Mr Thaçi. The details revealed in the new documents might cheer the prime minister, as they appear to shift responsibility from his shoulders to Mr Haradinaj's.

But as the evidence they contain was not used in Mr Haradinaj's original war crimes trial, it seems likely that prosecutors felt they were unable to stand up the claims. Moreover, Mr Haradinaj's name does not appear in Mr Marty's report. The situation remains murky.

The EU's [European Union's] police and justice mission in Kosovo, EULEX, is to investigate Mr Marty's claims, which go far beyond those of organ trafficking. But the new documents are unlikely to help in the search for justice. One well-placed source says that the hunt is already on in Kosovo to identify the witnesses.

After the leaks, anyone with knowledge of these events is unlikely to testify unless they receive guarantees of protection for years to come, including new identities and relocation abroad. That is a tragedy.

Everyone needs to know, once and for all, where the truth lies in this story, not least the families of the disappeared, as well as Kosovars whose leaders are now increasingly isolated internationally—in part thanks to these allegations.

China Is Harvesting the Organs of Executed Prisoners

Ethan Gutmann

Ethan Gutmann is an author and journalist. In the following viewpoint, he investigates allegations that China is selling the organs of Falun Gong prisoners to rich foreign nationals and Chinese residents. Even more shocking, says Gutmann, are charges that doctors are harvesting the organs when the patients are still alive. Gutmann points out that China does not legally recognize brain death, meaning that doctors routinely harvest the organs of death-row prisoners while their hearts are still beating. He also argues that one of the problems is that many in the human rights community question the credibility of Falun Gong practitioners and suggest that many of the more egregious charges might be exaggerated.

As you read, consider the following questions:

1. According to the author, when did the first allegations of large-scale organ harvesting of Falun Gong prisoners in China emerge?
2. When did China pass a law forbidding the sale of organs without the consent of the donor?

Ethan Gutmann, "China's Gruesome Organ Harvest," *Weekly Standard*, November 24, 2008. Copyright © 2008 by The Weekly Standard. All rights reserved. Reproduced by permission.

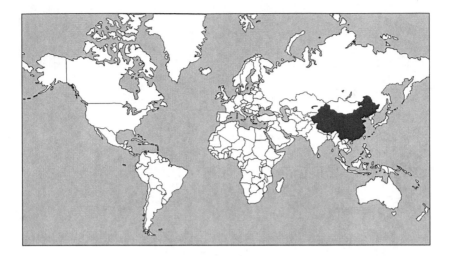

3. What percentage of transplanted kidneys in 2004 were donated by relatives, according to a Chinese report?

The jeepney driver sizes us up the minute we climb in. My research assistant is a healthy, young Israeli dude, so I must be the one with the money. He addresses his broken English to me: "Girl?"

No. No girls. Take us to the . . .

"Ladyboy? Kickboxer?"

No. No ladyboy, no kickboxer, thanks. I may be a paunchy, sweaty, middle-aged white guy, but I'm here to—well, actually, I am on my way to meet a Chinese woman in a back alley. She is going to tell me intimate stories of humiliation, torture, and abuse. And the truly shameful part is that after 50 or so interviews with refugees from Chinese labor camps, I won't even be listening that closely.

I'm in Bangkok because practitioners of Falun Gong, the Buddhist revival movement outlawed by Beijing, tend to head south when they escape from China. Those without passports make their way through Burma on motorcycles and back roads. Some have been questioned by U.N. [United Nations] case workers, but few have been interviewed by the press, even though, emerging from Chinese labor camps, they are eager, even desperate, to tell their stories. With the back-alley Chinese woman, I intend to direct my questions away from what she'll want to talk about—persecution and spirituality—to something she will barely remember, a seemingly innocuous part of her experience: a needle jab, some poking around the abdomen, an X-ray, a urine sample—medical tests consistent with assessment of prisoners for organ harvesting.

A Terrible Crime

My line of inquiry began in a Montreal community center over a year ago, listening to a heavy-set, middle-aged Chinese man named Wang Xiaohua, a soft-spoken ordinary guy except for the purple discoloration that extends down his forehead.

He recalled a scene: About 20 male Falun Gong practitioners were standing before the empty winter fields, flanked by two armed escorts. Instead of leading them out to dig up rocks and spread fertilizer, the police had rounded them up for some sort of excursion. It almost felt like a holiday. Wang had never seen most of the prisoners' faces before. Here in Yunnan Forced Labor Camp No. 2, Falun Gong detainees were carefully kept to a minority in each cell so that the hardened criminals could work them over.

Practitioners of Falun Gong were forbidden to communicate openly. Yet as the guards motioned for them to begin walking, Wang felt the group fall into step like a gentle migrating herd. He looked down at the red earth, streaked with straw and human waste, to the barren mountains on the horizon. Whatever lay ahead, Wang knew they were not afraid.

After 20 minutes, he saw a large gleaming structure in the distance—maybe it was a hospital, Wang thought. The summer of 2001 had been brutal in South China. After he'd worked for months in the burning sun, Wang's shaved head had become deeply infected. Perhaps it was getting a little better. Or perhaps he had just become used to it; lately he only noticed the warm, rancid stench of his rotting scalp when he woke up.

Wang broke the silence, asking one of the police guards if that was the camp hospital ahead. The guard responded evenly: "You know, we care so much about you. So we are taking you to get a physical. Look how well the party treats you. Normally, this kind of thing never happens in a labor camp."

Inside the facility, the practitioners lined up and, one by one, had a large blood sample drawn. Then a urine sample, electrocardiogram, abdominal X-ray, and eye exam. When Wang pointed to his head, the doctor mumbled something about it being normal and motioned for the next patient. Walking back to camp, the prisoners felt relieved, even a tad cocky, about the whole thing. In spite of all the torture they had endured and the brutal conditions, even the government would be forced to see that practitioners of Falun Gong were healthy.

They never did learn the results of any of those medical tests, Wang says, a little smile suddenly breaking through. He can't help it. He survived.

The charges [of organ harvesting] set off a quiet storm in the human rights community, yet the charge was not far-fetched.

Persistent Allegations

I spoke with Wang in 2007, just one out of over 100 interviews for a book on the clash between Falun Gong and the Chinese state. Wang's story is not new. Two prominent Canadian human rights attorneys, David Kilgour and David Matas, outlined his case and many others in their "Report into Allegations of Organ Harvesting of Falun Gong Practitioners in China," published and posted on the web in 2006.

By interviewing Wang, I was tipping my hat to the extensive research already done by others. I was not expecting to see Wang's pattern repeated as my interviews progressed, nor did I expect to find that organ harvesting had spread beyond Falun Gong. I was wrong.

A Brutal Campaign Against the Falun Gong

Falun Gong became wildly popular in China during the late 1990s. For various reasons—perhaps because the membership of this movement was larger than that of the Chinese Communist Party (and intersected with it), or because the legacy of Tiananmen was unresolved, or because 70 million people suddenly seemed to be looking for a way into heaven (other than money)—the party decided to eliminate it. In 1998, the party quietly canceled the business licenses of people who practiced Falun Gong. In 1999 came mass arrests, seizure of assets, and torture. Then, starting in 2000, as the movement responded by becoming more openly activist, demonstrating at Tiananmen and hijacking television signals on the mainland, the death toll started to climb, reaching approximately 3,000 confirmed deaths by torture, execution, and neglect by 2005.

At any given time, 100,000 Falun Gong practitioners were said to be somewhere in the Chinese penal system. Like most numbers coming out of China, these were crude estimates, further rendered unreliable by the chatter of claim and counterclaim. But one point is beyond dispute: The repression of Falun Gong spun out of control. Arrests, sentencing, and whatever took place in the detention centers, psychiatric institutions, and labor camps were not following any established legal procedure or restraint. As an act of passive resistance, or simply to avoid trouble for their families, many Falun Gong began withholding their names from the police, identifying themselves simply as "practitioner" or "Dafa disciple." When asked for their home province, they would say "the universe." For these, the nameless ones, whose families had no way of tracing them or agitating on their behalf, there may be no records at all.

In early 2006, the first charges of large-scale harvesting— surgical removal of organs while the prisoners were still alive, though of course the procedure killed them—of Falun Gong emerged from northeast China. The charges set off a quiet storm in the human rights community, yet the charge was not far-fetched.

An Open Secret

Harry Wu, a Chinese dissident who established the Laogai [Research] Foundation, had already produced reams of evidence that the state, after executing criminals formally sentenced to death, was selling their kidneys, livers, corneas, and other body parts to Chinese and foreigners, anyone who could pay the price. The practice started in the mid-1980s. By the mid-1990s, with the use of anti-tissue-rejection drugs pioneered by China, the business had progressed. Mobile organ-harvesting vans run by the armed services were routinely parked just outside the killing grounds to ensure that the military hospitals got first pick. This wasn't top secret. I spoke with a former Chinese police officer, a simple man from the countryside, who said that, as a favor to a condemned man's friend, he had popped open the back of such a van and unzipped the body bag. The corpse's chest had been picked clean.

Taiwanese doctors who arranged for patients to receive transplants on the mainland claim that there was no oversight of the system, no central Chinese database of organs and medical histories of donors, no red tape to diminish medical profits. So the real question was, at $62,000 for a fresh kidney, why would Chinese hospitals waste any body they could get their hands on?

Chinese Repression of the Falun Gong

[Chinese] authorities renewed the campaign to "transform" Falun Gong practitioners, which required prison and detention centres to force Falun Gong inmates to renounce their beliefs. Those considered "stubborn," that is, those who refuse to sign a statement to this effect, are typically tortured until they cooperate; many die in detention or shortly after release. . . .

Human rights lawyers were particularly susceptible to punishment by the authorities for taking on Falun Gong cases, including losing their licences, harassment and criminal prosecution.

- Guo Xiaojun, a former lecturer at a Shanghai university and a Falun Gong practitioner, was detained in Shanghai in January and later charged with "using a heretical organization to subvert the law". He was sentenced to four years in prison for allegedly having distributed Falun Gong materials. He was tortured in detention, kept in solitary confinement and eventually signed a confession that was used to uphold his sentence at a closed appeal hearing. . . .

- Lawyers Tang Jitian and Liu Wei had their licences permanently revoked in April by the Beijing Municipal Justice Bureau, on grounds of "disrupting the order of the court and interfering with the regular litigation process". The two had represented a Falun Gong practitioner in April 2009 in Sichuan province.

"Annual Report 2011:
The State of the World's Human Rights,"
Amnesty International, 2011.

An Unbelievable Charge

Yet what initially drew most fire from skeptics was the claim that organs were being harvested from people before they died. For all the Falun Gong theatrics, this claim was not so outlandish either. Any medical expert knows that a recipient is far less likely to reject a live organ; and any transplant dealer will confirm that buyers will pay more for one. Until recently, high volume Chinese transplant centers openly advertised the use of live donors on their websites.

It helps that brain death is not legally recognized in China; only when the heart stops beating is the patient actually considered dead. That means doctors can shoot a prisoner in the head, as it were, surgically, then remove the organs before the heart stops beating. Or they can administer anesthesia, remove the organs, and when the operation is nearing completion introduce a heart-stopping drug—the latest method. Either way, the prisoner has been executed, and harvesting is just fun along the way. In fact, according to doctors I have spoken to recently, all well versed in current mainland practices, live-organ harvesting of death-row prisoners in the course of execution is routine.

The real problem was that the charges came from Falun Gong—always the unplanned child of the dissident community. Unlike the Tiananmen student leaders and other Chinese prisoners of conscience who had settled into Western exile, Falun Gong marched to a distinctly Chinese drum. With its roots in a spiritual tradition from the Chinese heartland, Falun Gong would never have built a version of the Statue of Liberty and paraded it around for CNN. Indeed, to Western observers, Falun Gong public relations carried some of the uncouthness of Communist Party culture: a perception that practitioners tended to exaggerate, to create torture tableaux straight out of a Cultural Revolution opera, to spout slogans rather than facts.

For various reasons, some valid, some shameful, the credibility of persecuted refugees has often been doubted in the West. In 1939, a British Foreign Office official, politely speaking for the majority, described the Jews as not, perhaps, entirely reliable witnesses. During the Great Leap Forward, emaciated refugees from the mainland poured into Hong Kong, yammering about deserted villages and cannibalism. Sober Western journalists ignored these accounts as subjective and biased.

The yammering of a spiritual revivalist apparently counts for even less than the testimony of a peasant or a Jew. Thus, when Falun Gong unveiled a doctor's wife who claimed that her husband, a surgeon, had removed thousands of corneas from practitioners in a northeastern Chinese hospital named Sujiatun, the charge met with guarded skepticism from the dissident community and almost complete silence from the Western press (with the exception of this magazine and *National Review*).

Any medical expert knows that a recipient is far less likely to reject a live organ; and any transplant dealer will confirm that buyers will pay more for one. Until recently, high volume Chinese transplant centers openly advertised the use of live donors on their websites.

Gathering Evidence

As Falun Gong committees kicked into full investigative mode, the Canadian lawyers Kilgour and Matas compiled the accumulating evidence in their report. It included transcripts of recorded phone calls in which Chinese doctors confirmed that their organ donors were young, healthy, and practiced Falun Gong; written testimony from the mainland of practitioners' experiences in detention; an explosion in organ transplant activity coinciding with a rise in the Falun Gong incarceration rate, with international customers waiting as little as a week for a tissue match (in most countries, patients waited over a year). Finally, Kilgour and Matas compared the execution rate in China (essentially constant, according to Amnesty International) and the number of transplants. It left a discrepancy of 41,500 unexplained cases over a five-year span.

This report has never been refuted point by point, yet the vast majority of human rights activists have kept their distance. Since Falun Gong's claims were suspect, their allies' assertions were suspect. Transplant doctors who claimed to have Falun Gong organ donors in the basement? They were just saying what potential organ recipients wanted to hear. Written testimony from practitioners? They'd been prepped by activists. The rise in organ transplant activity? Maybe just better reporting. The discrepancy between executions and transplants? As a respected human rights scholar asked me, why did Kilgour and Matas use Amnesty International's estimate of the number of executions in China to suggest the execution rate had stayed constant for 10 years? Even Amnesty acknowledges their numbers might represent a gross understatement. There might be no discrepancy at all.

Finally, why had no real witness, a doctor or nurse who had actually operated on Falun Gong practitioners, come forward? Without such proof (although such an individual's credibility can always be savaged, even with supporting documents), human rights advocates argued there was no reason to take the story seriously. There certainly were not sufficient grounds for President [George W.] Bush to mention organ harvesting in his human rights speech on the eve of the Beijing Olympics [in the summer of 2008].

A New Law

The critics had hinted at legitimate points of discussion. But so had the Chinese government: Fresh off the confession in 2005 that organs were being harvested from ordinary death-row prisoners, and after issuing their predictable denials of harvesting organs from Falun Gong, Beijing suddenly passed a law in July 2006 for bidding the sale of organs without the consent of the donor.

Three things happened. The organ supply tightened. Prices doubled. And transplants continued. So unless there has been a dramatic cultural shift since 2004, when a Chinese report found that only 1.5 percent of transplanted kidneys were donated by relatives, the organs being sold must still come from somewhere. Let's assume it's prisoners—that's what Taiwanese doctors think—and theorize that the new law was a signal: Get your consent forms and stop harvesting from Falun Gong. For now.

And the critics had one thing exactly right: Precision is an illusion. No taped conversation with a mainland doctor is unimpeachable. All witnesses from China have mixed motives, always. And, again, no numbers from China, even the one in the last paragraph, can be considered definitive.

Indeed, the entire investigation must be understood to be still at an early, even primitive, stage. We do not really know the scale of what is happening yet. Think of 1820, when a handful of doctors, scientists, and amateur fossil hunters were trying to make sense of scattered suggestive evidence and a disjointed pile of bones. Twenty-two years would pass before an English paleontologist so much as coined the term "dinosaur"—"terrible lizard"—and the modern study of these extinct creatures got seriously under way. Those of us researching the harvesting of organs from involuntary donors in China are like the early dinosaur hunters. We don't work in close consultation with each other. We are still waiting for even one doctor who has harvested organs from living prisoners of conscience to emerge from the mainland. Until that happens, it is true, we don't even have dinosaur bones. But we do have tracks. Here are some that I've found.

Qu's Story

Qu Yangyao, an articulate Chinese professional, holds three master's degrees. She is also the earliest refugee to describe an "organs only" medical examination. Qu escaped to Sydney last year [2007]. While a prisoner in China in June 2000, she refused to "transform"—to sign a statement rejecting Falun Gong—and was eventually transferred to a labor camp. Qu's health was fairly good, though she had lost some weight from hunger strikes. Given Qu's status and education, there were reasons to keep her healthy. The Chinese police wanted to avoid deaths in custody—less paperwork, fewer questions. At least, so Qu assumed.

Qu was 35 years old when the police escorted her and two other practitioners into a hospital. Qu distinctly remembers the drawing of a large volume of blood, then a chest X-ray, and probing. "I wasn't sure what it was about. They just touch you in different places . . . abdomen, liver." She doesn't remember giving a urine sample at that time, but the doctor did shine a light in her eyes, examining her corneas.

Did the doctor then ask her to trace the movement of his light with her eyes, or check her peripheral vision? No. He just checked her corneas, skipping any test involving brain function. And that was it: no hammer on the knee, no feeling for lymph nodes, no examination of ears or mouth or genitals—the doctor checked her retail organs and nothing else.

I may have felt a silent chill run up my spine at points in our interview, but Qu, like many educated subjects, seemed initially unaware of the potential implications of what she was telling me. Many prisoners preserve a kind of "it can't happen here" sensibility. "I'm too important to be wiped out" is the survivor's mantra. In the majority of the interviews . . . , my subjects, though aware of the organ harvesting issue, had no clear idea of my line of questioning or the "right" answers.

Falun Gong practitioners are forbidden to lie. That doesn't mean they never do. In the course of my interviews I've heard a few distortions. Not because people have been "prepped," but because they've suffered trauma. Deliberate distortions, though, are exceedingly rare. The best way to guard against false testimony is to rely on extended sit-down interviews.

In all, I interviewed 15 Falun Gong refugees from labor camps or extended detention who had experienced something inexplicable in a medical setting. My research assistant, Lee-shai Lemish, interviewed Dai Ying in Norway, bringing our total to 16. If that number seems low, consider the difficulty of survival and escape. Even so, just over half of the subjects can be ruled out as serious candidates for organ harvesting: too old, too physically damaged from hard labor, or too emaciated from hunger strikes. Some were simply too shaky in their recall of specific procedures to be much help to us. Some were the subjects of drug tests. Some received seemingly normal, comprehensive physicals, though even such people sometimes offered valuable clues.

Periodical and Internet Sources Bibliography

The following articles have been selected to supplement the diverse views presented in this chapter.

Arthur Caplan	"The Trouble with Organ Trafficking," Council for Secular Humanism, January 31, 2012. www.secularhumanism.org.
Emran Hossain and Kongkon Karmaker	"Doctors Played Dubious Role," *Daily Star* (Bangladesh), January 24, 2012.
Jeneen Interlandi	"Not Just Urban Legend," *Newsweek*, January 9, 2009.
Joel Millman and Matt Bradley	"Trafficking in Organs Said to Rise in Egypt," *Wall Street Journal*, December 12, 2011.
Dallia Moniem	"Organ Trafficking on the Rise in Post-Mubarak Egypt," Africa Review, January 10, 2012. www.africareview.com.
Michael Montgomery	"EU Endorses Task Force to Probe Organ Trafficking Allegations in Kosovo," Center for Investigative Reporting, June 9, 2011. http://cironline.org.
Gitonga Njeru	"Kenya: Sex-Trafficked Women and Girls Also Vulnerable to Organ Trafficking," Women News Network, September 13, 2011. http://womennewsnetwork.net.
Fred Pleitgen and Mohamed Fadel Fahmy	"Refugees Face Organ Theft in the Sinai," CNN.com, November 3, 2011.
David Smith	"South African Hospital Firm Admits 'Cash for Kidney' Transplants," *Guardian*, November 10, 2010.
Michael Smith, Daryna Krasnolutska, and David Glovin	"Organ Gangs Force Poor to Sell Kidneys for Desperate Israelis," *Bloomberg Markets Magazine*, November 1, 2011.

For Further Discussion

Chapter 1

1. Rates of organ donations vary widely from country to country—and even city to city. Based on the selections in this chapter, what makes some countries and regions more successful in organ donations? What makes others less successful?

Chapter 2

1. How do religious misconceptions affect organ donation rates in many countries? Utilize information from countries discussed in the viewpoints in this chapter to back up your answer.

2. In his viewpoint, Paul Voosen explores the controversy surrounding the emerging field of facial transplants. What is your opinion of the surgery? What steps do you think should be taken to address the apprehensions about the procedure?

Chapter 3

1. This chapter touches on several policies that are being implemented to raise organ donations in countries around the world. Which ones do you think can be successful in your community? Which ones do you think will have little effect on the rate, and why?

2. Many countries are considering implementing a presumed consent organ donation policy. What is your opinion on presumed consent? Would you support it in your community? Explain your answer.

Chapter 4

1. What policies can countries adopt to address organ trafficking? What factors need to be in place to stop organ trafficking?

2. Ethan Gutmann's viewpoint reports on China's harvesting of organs from death-row prisoners for organ transplantation. What are the ethical and moral issues involved with this practice? Is there any justification in favor of what China is doing? Explain your reasoning.

Organizations to Contact

The editors have compiled the following list of organizations concerned with the issues debated in this book. The descriptions are derived from materials provided by the organizations. All have publications or information available for interested readers. The list was compiled on the date of publication of the present volume; the information provided here may change. Be aware that many organizations take several weeks or longer to respond to inquiries, so allow as much time as possible.

American Society of Transplantation (AST)
15000 Commerce Parkway, Ste. C, Mt. Laurel, NJ   08054
(856) 439-9986 • fax: (856) 439-9982
website: www.a-s-t.org

The American Society of Transplantation (AST) is an international association of transplant professionals that promotes research, education, and advocacy about organ transplantation. AST offers a forum for professionals in the field to exchange and disseminate information on the latest research, equipment, techniques, and patient care. The AST website features a series of educational webcasts and podcasts for transplant professionals; a calendar of upcoming events, including lectures, seminars, and meetings; recent press releases, research, and patient education brochures; and issue briefs and position papers on subjects of interest in the field.

Canadian Society of Transplantation (CST)
774 Echo Drive, Ottawa, Ontario   K1S 5N8
   Canada
(613) 730-6274 • fax: (613) 730-1116
e-mail: cst@rcpsc.edu
website: www.cst-transplant.ca

The Canadian Society of Transplantation (CST) is Canada's organization of transplantation professionals. CST works to promote research and awareness of organ transplantation in

Canada and emphasizes education and the exchange of information on recent scientific progress in the field, especially in the area of patient care. The CST website provides access to *CST News*, a quarterly e-newsletter; upcoming events; and updates on research, CST initiatives, and government health policies that impact organ donation and transplantation. The website also offers webinars, press releases, and a range of other resources.

Donate Life America

701 E. Byrd Street, 16th Floor, Richmond, VA   23219
(804) 377-3580
e-mail: donatelifeamerica@donatelife.net
website: donatelife.net

Donate Life America is a nonprofit alliance of US organizations that work together to raise organ donation awareness and rates of registration across the country. It also manages Donate Life State Teams that work in states to facilitate donor registries; carry out effective donor education programs; and raise awareness of the need for organ and tissue donors. The Donate Life America website allows visitors to access their states' organ donor registries and to sign up to be a donor. It also offers stories of donors and recipients, as well as provides information on the donation process.

Donor Action Foundation

Prinsendreef 10, Linden   B-3210
   Belgium
+32 16 621469 • fax: +32 16 623443
e-mail: info@donoraction.org
website: www.donoraction.org

The Donor Action Foundation is an international alliance of leading donor and transplantation organizations working to increase organ and tissue donation rates; aid in developing donation processes and protocols; raise awareness of the Donor Action Program; and enhance and monitor donor family care. The Donor Action Program was created to help hospitals all over the world improve organ donation programs, processes, and protocols to help patients find the organs they need to survive and provide the hospitals with the resources, staff, and knowledge they need to effectively perform transplant operations. To that end, the Donor Action Foundation offers a series of e-classes for health professionals that provide information and opportunities in the donor transplantation field. The alliance's website also features news, listings of upcoming events, fact sheets, and a range of training materials and resources.

Global Organization for Organ Donation (GOOD)
PO Box 52757, Tulsa, OK 74105
(918) 605-1994 • fax: (918) 745-6637
e-mail: info@global-good.org
website: www.global-good.org

The Global Organization for Organ Donation (GOOD) is a nonprofit organization that is dedicated to "saving lives; raising awareness for organ, eye, and tissue donation; correcting misconceptions about donation and increasing the number of people willing to donate life." GOOD has initiated a newspaper campaign, "Circle of Life," which details the experiences of both donors and recipients to raise awareness about the need for and benefits of organ donation. These stories can be accessed on the GOOD website. Also available on the website are articles about the organization, information on resources, and a section addressing misconceptions about the organ donation process.

The National Network of Organ Donors (TNNOD)
PO Box 223613, West Palm Beach, FL 33422
866-577-9798
e-mail: info@tnnod.org
website: www.thenationalnetworkoforgandonors.org

The National Network of Organ Donors (TNNOD) is a nonprofit organization that strives to increase the number of organ donors in the United States by removing legal and emotional barriers that inhibit donors and families. One of TNNOD's key goals is to lobby legislators to pass laws to give "hospitals and doctors immunity from lawsuits in cases where a patient's intent to donate organs is being challenged by family members." Ultimately, TNNOD aims to remove the threat of liability from the organ donation process. The TNNOD website features updates on recent efforts, statistics on organ donation in the United States, and access to the TNNOD e-newsletter.

Transplant Recipients International Organization (TRIO)

2100 M Street NW, #170-353, Washington, DC   20037
(202) 293-0980
e-mail: info@trioweb.org
website: www.trioweb.org

The Transplant Recipients International Organization (TRIO) is a nonprofit organization that aims to help the families of organ, eye, and tissue donors and recipients and their families through increased awareness of the need for organ donation; supports increased access to resources; and effectively advocates for policies that streamline the process and respect the wishes of everyone involved in organ donation and transplantation. TRIO publishes a quarterly e-newsletter, *Lifelines*, which highlights recent events and activities, legislative and educational initiatives, and other information relevant in the transplant field.

The Transplantation Society (TTS)

1255 University Street, Ste. 605, Montreal, Quebec   H3B 3V9
   Canada
(514) 874-1717 • fax: (514) 874-1716
e-mail: info@tts.org
website: www.tts.org

The Transplantation Society (TTS) is an international association of transplantation professionals that strives to develop the science and clinical practice of organ and tissue donation; foster communication between professionals in the field; offer opportunities for continuing education; and guide members on effective ethical practices when it comes to transplantation. Above all, it is dedicated to be a global leader in the industry. One of the group's recent initiatives is to provide resources, including networking opportunities, for women. The Transplantation Society publishes a number of journals, including the *Transplantation Journal*, which is published twice monthly and covers the most important advances in the field. Every two years the society sponsors a World Congress, which brings together professionals from all over the world to exchange information about new research, clinical practices, and surgical techniques.

Transplantation Society of Australia and New Zealand (TSANZ)

145 Macquarie Street, Sydney, New South Wales   2000
    Australia
+61 2 9256 5461 • fax: +61 2 9241 4083
e-mail: tsanz@tsanz.com.au
website: www.tsanz.com.au

The Transplantation Society of Australia and New Zealand (TSANZ) is an association for transplantation professionals that works to develop protocols in donor eligibility and organ and tissue allocation. TSANZ also organizes meetings, conferences, seminars, and other opportunities for transplant professionals to gather and exchange information about such issues. It sponsors annual scientific conferences that feature experts in the field presenting new research and information on clinical practices and surgical techniques. TSANZ publishes a newsletter that provides updates on recent events and new protocols, policies, and practices.

United Network for Organ Sharing (UNOS)

PO Box 2484, Richmond, VA   23218
888-894-6361
website: www.unos.org

The United Network for Organ Sharing (UNOS) is the private organization that manages the US transplant system. UNOS describes its mission as "to advance organ availability and transplantation by uniting and supporting our communities for the benefit of patients through education, technology and policy development." UNOS coordinates the US organ transplant list and finds donor matches for patients; develops fair and effective transplantation policies; provides assistance to patients, transplant professionals, and donor families; and educates the public about the organ donor program. The UNOS website features statistics, fact sheets, information on current policies, and breaking news in the industry.

World Health Organization (WHO)
Avenue Appia 20, Geneva 27   1211
   Switzerland
(+41) 22 791 21 11 • fax: (+41) 22 791 31 11
e-mail: info@who.int
website: www.who.int

The World Health Organization (WHO) is the United Nations agency responsible for directing global health care matters. WHO funds research into health issues that affect global health, including the need for organ donation and organ transplantation. The agency monitors health trends, compiles useful statistics, and offers technical support to countries looking to boost rates of organ donations. The WHO website features podcasts, blogs, and videos; it also offers fact sheets, reports, studies, and a calendar of events. There are a broad range of articles on organ transplantation and organ donation on the website.

Bibliography of Books

Katrina A. Bramstedt and Rena Down — *The Organ Donor Experience: Good Samaritans and the Meaning of Altruism*. Lanham, MD: Rowman & Littlefield, 2011.

Scott Carney — *The Red Market: On the Trail of the World's Organ Brokers, Bone Thieves, Blood Farmers, and Child Traffickers*. New York: William Morrow, 2011.

Steve Farber and Harlan Abrahams — *On the List: Fixing America's Failing Organ Transplant System*. New York: Macmillan, 2009.

Anne-Maree Farrell, David Price, and Muireann Quigley, eds. — *Organ Shortage: Ethics, Law, and Pragmatism*. New York: Cambridge University Press, 2011.

Reg Green — *The Gift That Heals: Stories of Hope, Renewal and Transformation Through Organ and Tissue Donation*. Bloomington, IN: AuthorHouse, 2007.

Petr T. Grinkovskiy, ed. — *Organ Donation: Supply, Policies and Practices*. New York: Nova Science, 2009.

Sherine Hamdy — *Our Bodies Belong to God: Organ Transplants, Islam, and the Struggle for Human Dignity in Egypt*. Berkeley: University of California Press, 2012.

David Hamilton *A History of Organ Transplantation: Ancient Legends to Modern Practice.* Pittsburgh, PA: University of Pittsburgh Press, 2012.

D. Scott Henderson *Death and Donation: Rethinking Brain Death as a Means for Procuring Transplantable Organs.* Eugene, OR: Pickwick Publications, 2011.

Steven J. Jensen *The Ethics of Organ Transplantation.* Washington, DC: Catholic University of America Press, 2011.

Susan E. Lederer *Flesh and Blood: Organ Transplantation and Blood Transfusion in Twentieth-Century America.* New York: Oxford University Press, 2008.

Sheila A.M. McLean *Autonomy, Consent and the Law.* New York: Routledge-Cavendish, 2010.

Franklin G. Miller and Robert D. Truog *Death, Dying, and Organ Transplantation: Reconstructing Medical Ethics at the End of Life.* Oxford, UK: Oxford University Press, 2012.

Farhat Moazam *Bioethics and Organ Transplantation in a Muslim Society: A Study in Culture, Ethnography, and Religion.* Bloomington: Indiana University Press, 2006.

Graciela Nowenstein *The Generosity of the Dead: A Sociology of Organ Procurement in France.* Burlington, VT: Ashgate, 2010.

David Price — *Human Tissue in Transplantation and Research: A Model Legal and Ethical Donation Network.* New York: Cambridge University Press, 2010.

Aslihan Sanal — *New Organs Within Us: Transplants and the Moral Economy.* Durham, NC: Duke University Press, 2011.

Thomas Schlich — *The Origins of Organ Transplantation: Surgery and Laboratory Science, 1880–1930.* Rochester, NY: University of Rochester Press, 2010.

Jason T. Siegel and Eusebio M. Alvaro, eds — *Understanding Organ Donation: Applied Behavioral Science Perspectives.* Chichester, UK: Wiley-Blackwell, 2010.

Daniel Sperling — *Posthumous Interests: Legal and Ethical Perspectives.* New York: Cambridge University Press, 2008.

Leonard Territo and Rande Matteson, eds. — *The International Trafficking of Human Organs: A Multidisciplinary Perspective.* Boca Raton, FL: Taylor & Francis, 2011.

David L. Weimer — *Medical Governance: Values, Expertise, and Interests in Organ Transplantation.* Washington, DC: Georgetown University Press, 2010.

T.M. Wilkinson — *Ethics and the Acquisition of Organs.* Oxford, UK: Oxford University Press, 2011.

Index

Geographic headings and page numbers in **boldface** refer to viewpoints about that country or region.

Brain death
  cultural variability in acceptance of, 65
  Israeli debates about acceptance of, 95–96, 98
  Japanese donor data, 103
  Japan's support for concept of, 42
Brauer, Karl, 16
Brazil
  global trafficking in, 165, 168
  international organ trade, 28
  kidney sales, 30
  underground market for organs, 123
British Medical Journal, 135
British National Health Service, 56, 139
Buddhism, 88
Buddhism beliefs about organ donation, 42, 90
Burnet, Frank, 17

C

Cain, Patrick, 61–66
Canada, 61–66, 120–127
  black market demands and pricing, 122
  booming transplant market in, 121–122
  demand for kidneys, 175
  exploitation risks, 126
  illegality of profits from donation, 123
  incentives for suppliers, 122–123
  kidney transplant data, 31
  monitoring strategies, 126–127
  moral considerations, 123–125
  offsetting costs to taxpayers, 125

  Ontario's variable donations rate, 61–66
  organ imports, 31
  Organs Watch report, 31
  recommendation for paying organ donors, 120–127
  renal transplants data, 31
  risks vs. rewards, 125–126
  suspected kidney agents in, 174
Canadian Blood Services, 122, 126–127
Caplan, Arthur, 110
Carney, Scott, 150–155
Carrell, Alexis, 17
Catholic Church position on organ donation, 90
Charity Association for the Support of Kidney Patients (CASKP), 168
Charity Foundation for Special Diseases (CFSD), 168
China, 195–207
  curtailment of international trade, 30
  executed prisoner organ harvesting, 195–207
  face transplant attempt, 106
  illegal organ trade, 184
  kidney, liver transplant data, 30
  transplant tourism, 27
  underground market for organs, 123
Cholia, Ami, 164–168
Christian Medical College (India), 178
Church of Jesus Christ of Latter-Day Saints, 93–94
Clinical Procedures Unit (Department of Essential Health Technologies, WHO), 25
Cohen, Lawrence, 167

CPSIA information can be obtained
at www.ICGtesting.com
Printed in the USA
FFOW02n0952300114
3346FF